THIRD EDITION

Cases in Emotional and Behavioral Disorders of Children and Youth

James M. Kauffman

University of Virginia, Emeritus

Timothy J. Landrum

University of Louisville

Boston   Columbus   Indianapolis   New York   San Francisco   Upper Saddle River
Amsterdam   Cape Town   Dubai   London   Madrid   Milan   Munich   Paris   Montreal   Toronto
Delhi   Mexico City   São Paulo   Sydney   Hong Kong   Seoul   Singapore   Taipei   Tokyo

Executive Editor & Publisher: Stephen D. Dragin
Editorial Assistant: Katherine Wiley
Marketing Manager: Joanna Sabella
Production Editor: Mary Beth Finch
Production Manager: Laura Messerly
Cover Designer: Suzanne Duda
Cover Art: Shutterstock
Full-Service Project Management: Dhanya Ramesh, Jouve
Composition: Jouve India
Printer/Binder: Courier/Westford
Cover Printer: Courier/Westford
Text Font: 10/12 Janson Text LT Std

Credits and acknowledgments for materials borrowed from other sources and reproduced, with permission, in this textbook appear on appropriate page within text.

Library of Congress Cataloging-in-Publication Data
Kauffman, James M.
  Cases in emotional and behavioral disorders of children and youth / James
M. Kauffman, Timothy J. Landrum. — 3rd ed.
      p. cm.
  Includes bibliographical references.
  ISBN 978-0-13-268466-8
  1. Behavior disorders in children—Case studies.   2. Affective disorders
in children—Case studies.   I. Landrum, Timothy J.   II. Title.

  RJ506.B44K378 2013
  618.92'89—dc23

                                        2012005802

10 9 8 7 6 5 4 3 2 1   V013

ISBN 10: 0-13-268466-7
ISBN 13: 978-0-13-268466-8

CONTENTS

PREFACE

This casebook contains cases that we have garnered from our reading of both popular and professional literature and from personal contacts with individuals who have confronted difficult or disturbing behavior in their roles as parents, teachers, or adult members of a community. We have written our own descriptions of the cases: for the most part, these are based on published accounts or on our own experience (or both). A select number of the cases were written specifically for this book by someone else, whom we credit as the source. In all instances, we have kept the facts of the case similar to those depicted elsewhere if the case was described in the literature.

The cases are grouped by topic. Instructors or students, however, may find that a given case has conceptual links to more than one topic. This is as it should be, as emotional and behavioral disorders are not phenomena that can be packaged neatly into a single category.

Although the cases are grouped by specific topics (book chapters), most of them could bear revisiting as a student progresses through coursework. Some of the questions about the cases, and some questions an instructor might want to ask or a student might pose, may have no fixed answer. Moreover, the "answers" might change after further study and research of the problem or topic area.

We have provided a brief introduction for each case. We have also suggested questions that could be discussed in class or answered in writing, or both. The questions we pose are by no means the only ones of importance, and we encourage instructors and/or students to formulate their own questions about the cases.

We hope this casebook will enrich and enliven any course in which it is used. Our hope is that studying these cases will help prepare the individuals who read them to work more effectively with young people who have such disorders.

New to the Third Edition

In this edition of the casebook, we have made some significant changes:

- We have changed the order and designation of the chapter titles to correspond to the text we prepared in its tenth edition, *Characteristics of Emotional and Behavioral Disorders of Children and Youth*.
- We have moved five interviews to this casebook from the personal reflections written by teachers for the ninth edition of the textbook. These are interviews of students having particular disorders.

- We have written six new cases specifically for this casebook.
- We have deleted five cases that we had included in the second edition and changed names in several others.
- We have also edited and updated the introduction to this casebook, "The Use of Cases," to reflect recent literature and say with greater precision what we hope this casebook will accomplish.

New! CourseSmart eTextbook Available

CourseSmart is an exciting new choice for students looking to save money. As an alternative to purchasing the printed textbook, students can purchase an electronic version of the same content. With a CourseSmart eTextbook, students can search the text, make notes online, print out reading assignments that incorporate lecture notes, and bookmark important passages for later review. For more information, or to purchase access to the CourseSmart eTextbook, visit www.coursesmart.com.

Acknowledgments

We would like to thank the reviewers for this edition: Kathy Fejes, Drake University; Dr. Erik Greene, University of Georgia; Dr. Michelle J. McCollin, Slippery Rock University; and Robert J. Stansberry, Carroll College.

James M. Kauffman
Timothy J. Landrum

THE USE OF CASES

Cases can be an important teaching tool in many professional fields, including medicine, nursing, business, and, more recently, education. The basic idea is that students preparing to enter a given field can learn a great deal more by reading and thinking about actual problems, not merely reading the usual text material alone (e.g., Goor and Santos, 2002; Kauffman, Pullen, Mostert, and Trent, 2011). The text material may be important in providing basic concepts that cases alone do not provide, but the cases provide complex examples that give students practice in applying the concepts.

Thus, cases usually are not meant to be used without a textbook that presents concepts in the typical expository or academic manner. They are meant to amplify concepts presented in a text, provide a scenario in which the concepts can be applied to real-life problems, and prompt deeper thinking and further questioning by students.

Of course, a case never provides all the information anyone could want or ask for. But in actual practice as well, professionals often must make judgments or decisions without having all the information they would like to have. Sometimes it is wise to wait for more information, but in some circumstances the practitioner can't wait. Cases always demand that readers do two things: (1) make a judgment based on the information provided, and (2) ask questions for which answers are not provided. The following is always an important question: "What would you do, given the information we have?" Another important question, however, is, "Suppose we find out that _____, then what would you do?" The "Suppose . . ." requires asking additional questions in light of what is already known about the case. In essence, we want students to think like scientists, to be skeptical, to ask questions and look for data-based answers (see Kauffman, 2011).

Instructors may use cases in a variety of ways. They may ask students to read a case and be ready to discuss it in class. But they may ask students to write answers to questions about the case, pose additional questions about the case, or use some combination of these or other tactics. The questions following each case are merely a beginning point for reflection on the meaning of the behavior and proposed responses to it. In fact, we hope that students reading the cases will think of many other important questions to ask.

1

Case on Where to Begin

Here is the story of a mother's two sons, John and his older brother. Both were students with attention deficit hyperactivity disorder (ADHD). John, however, had additional problems. The case was written by Cindy Ahler, John's mother. It raises many questions about where to begin—how an emotional or behavioral disorder (EBD) in its many manifestations might best be conceptualized and managed.

John

I always considered myself lucky. I had grown up in a very loving family. I always wanted to get married and be a mother and wife. I got married a year out of high school and had three children. Then I got pregnant with a fourth child, and somehow knew things would never be the same.

My oldest and third children were delightful but very active girls, and my middle child was a boy who had been difficult to deal with behaviorally. He, however, was a wonderfully bright and loving child. I sought out help early on, and eventually he was diagnosed as having ADHD. He was on Ritalin by the time he entered kindergarten and was doing quite well in school.

My pregnancy with John was pretty miserable overall because I did not feel well, either physically or psychologically. John was born two days before Christmas by cesarean section. So, for the first time, I had to be away from my children and husband over the holidays. In utero, John was extraordinarily active, causing me a great deal of pain and discomfort. It did not take long to discover that he was a very different infant and child. Looking back on it, I can see now that he was born angry.

John's growth and development were relatively normal for the first couple of years. He reached his cognitive and motor milestones pretty much on target. He, however, was fairly irritable and definitely hyperactive. There had been problems in my marriage before John was born, but another child with behavioral issues was the final blow. John's father and I separated when John was about 18 months old.

John's irritability and hyperactivity were so difficult to deal with during this stressful time that I took him to see a pediatrician to see whether we could get the ADHD diagnosis and put him on Ritalin. With Ritalin, we could avoid a lot of the problems I had had with his older brother, Robert. After observing John for about four to five minutes, she declared that he was a normal child and the real problem was that I was not coping with the breakup of my marriage. She sent us to family therapy.

The consensus at that time was that if there was a problem with a child, there was a problem with the family and with parenting techniques.

Neighbors and relatives had been quick to advise me to take a firmer hand with my boys—"Take John to the shed for a whipping a couple of times and he'll shape up," they suggested. I never believed in corporal punishment, but I did believe in setting firm limits. Indeed, I had learned a lot about parenting because of the problems I had with my oldest son. I read every book imaginable and went to many workshops and talks given about parenting children with behavioral problems. Many of the ideas were helpful with my other son but did little to improve things with John. My oldest boy was doing well enough with Ritalin, and I wanted the same for John.

I was having great difficulty keeping daycare providers for John because of his behavior. Eventually, I took John to the same place I had taken his older brother when he was finally diagnosed with ADHD. There, I met with a team of people—a couple of psychologists and a pediatric nurse practitioner, who were employed by the public school district to evaluate children in the school district who were having behavioral and learning problems. It did not take them long to decide that John also had ADHD. Armed with their evaluation, I was able to get a different pediatrician to put John on Ritalin. The Ritalin did help somewhat, but not as much as it had helped his older brother.

John's birthday is in December, so he entered kindergarten just shy of his sixth birthday. He went to the same private K–8 elementary school as his older siblings had attended. His teacher was older than most and very exacting. At the end of the year she decided it would be better for him if I kept him in kindergarten another year because of his behavior, even though he was functioning at grade level academically. I chose not to do this because I felt his self-esteem would suffer. The next year, his first-grade teacher was enthusiastic but not very experienced. She believed that he was not capable of keeping up with the other students academically and that he did have difficulty with peer relationships. According to national standards, however, John's skills were still at grade level. At this school, most of the children operated substantially above grade level, which placed him near the bottom of his class. She would not pass him on to the next grade, and the principal stood behind her decision. I decided that rather than keeping him back I would send him to public school.

The local public school was very different from the private school. He had a second-grade teacher who could not control her classroom at all. At the end of that year, according to the standardized tests, John had not gained any ground in his reading and math skills and so was a year behind where he should have been. I returned him to his former school the following year. There, the new principal assured me that we could all work together and achieve success for John.

John started third grade with new resolve. Early on, I attempted to form a partnership with his teacher to help John be successful. She, however, made it abundantly clear to me that at this age she expected John to remember to go get his medications at lunchtime and to copy down and do his assignments without prompting from her. She told me that the only way to get him to act responsibly was to hold high expectations and punish him when he failed to meet those expectations. John was still having difficulty with peer relationships as well. He was very small for his age and looked immature. He had a very hot temper. The other children teased him endlessly, and he was frequently in trouble for fighting. One day on the playground, two children were teasing him, and he swung his backpack at them. His teacher saw him do it. During homeroom period, she took him out into the hallway and slapped him across the face, nearly knocking him over. This was witnessed by several of his fellow classmates, and I only heard about it later when several parents called to tell me. Their own children had come home from school and were very upset about their teacher's behavior. Because there were only a couple of weeks left in the school year, I kept him home and did schoolwork with him there.

The next year I was able to petition to get him into a different public school, one that was known for working well with children with ADHD. He did struggle, but he did relatively well that year despite some new problems. At this time, John was discovered to have a deficiency in growth hormone and began having daily growth hormone injections. Over the course of this year, there were weeks at a time when he would be a virtual recluse. He would come home from school, turn off all the lights, close the drapes, and sit two feet from the television, almost in a trance. He was particularly irritable at these times, and if friends called to ask him to come out and play, he would not even talk to them on the phone. He had difficulty getting to sleep at night, and it was difficult for him to get up for school in the morning. Eventually, he began to tell me how much he wanted to die because he hated his life. He began displaying some self-injurious behavior. We consulted a child psychiatrist, and John was eventually admitted to the children's mental health unit at the local hospital. They tried some anticonvulsant medications (then the standard treatment for bipolar disorder), and his mood and behavior began to improve. Then he developed a severe allergic reaction to the drug he was taking and to other medications in that drug category. The psychiatrist would not diagnose bipolar disorder, which both John's pediatrician and I now suspected was his problem. Instead, the psychiatrist diagnosed him as having oppositional defiant disorder (ODD) and ADHD. The psychiatrist told me that I simply could not allow John to behave this way and that I had to set firmer limits on his behavior. I must make John be responsible for his own behavior. He said I was looking for the "magic" pill and there was not one.

In the fall of the next academic year, on one of the few occasions when he played outside, he jumped out of a tree about 20 feet off the ground and shattered his ankle. This required surgery to repair and casting that lasted three months. His behavior began to take on a different pattern. In the fall and spring, he had periods when he was extremely hyperactive and displayed a volatile temper. Then in the winter, he would be reclusive, generally irritable, and very emotional, with multiple episodes of uncontrollable sobbing. It was during these times that he would do things to injure himself. His endocrinologist thought he might have a seasonal affective disorder. Then John's behavior pattern changed again. The periods of time with depressive-like symptoms and the hyperactivity seemed to occur during both winter and spring, which would be inconsistent with seasonal affective disorder.

At the end of sixth grade, John's teachers passed him on despite the fact that he really was nonfunctional in school. They told me that he needed to get into a special education program especially designed for children with behavioral problems.

He went to the public junior high in the fall and was placed in a special education program. In this program, there were children who had behavior problems, but they were all very different problems from John. Many had been in trouble with the law. They had stolen cars, vandalized property, were truant from school, or had been in trouble with illegal drugs. Most had significant problems in their families. In order to fit in with the group, John had to become more like them. He began to be disrespectful to me, curse and swear, and be much more defiant to authority figures. When we found medications that would adequately quiet John, he became so sleepy that he could not stay awake at school. If we did not medicate him, he became volatile and was locked in the school's "time-out" room, which was basically a padded cell. We endured two more years of this. As before, he was passed to the next grade, even though he was getting next to nothing out of school.

The junior high experience was also very isolating for John socially. I could not let him visit any of his friends from school at their homes because the environments were so bad. He was allowed to bring friends home, but his friends stole some of John's prized possessions. John was crushed and didn't understand this. Of course his behavior was too strange even for them, and they would beat him up. He had to learn to put on a very tough exterior and become even more like them just to survive.

Senior high was even worse than junior high. That is when I began to realize that John was smoking marijuana and suspected there were other illegal drugs involved. School authorities expected more from him. They actually held the special education students to a much higher standard of behavior than the mainstream students. There were a million ways to get suspended from school, and John must have found at least half of them. In ninth grade, he spent more time suspended than he did attending school. More often than not, the school would only inform me of the suspension by mail several days after the fact rather than at the time it happened. In other words, he would be out running around during the day and I would think he was in school. It was during one of these many school suspensions that John jumped off the top of a bus stop and severely fractured both of the bones in his forearm. Life was constant turmoil.

This senior high school also had a policeman assigned to the school full time. Whenever there was a possibility to get the law involved, the school did. It became very clear to me that John was being warehoused in a school system that had no idea what to do except call the police. They did not want these children, and the consensus was that if these children could not behave properly, the teachers or administrators would find a way to have them locked up and sent away.

So I decided to move out to a rural area. I was convinced that getting John out of the city and away from the influence of the gang members who were his classmates was crucial. We moved about 40 miles out of the city to a neighboring rural county and were able to get a mental health case manager through this county almost immediately (John had been on a waiting list for three years in the county in which we had lived previously). I do believe that this social worker tried hard to be helpful, but I soon realized how limited those services were. She was able to get some assistance from an agency that provided after-school home care. By this time, John's mood swings were very wide, with frequent fluctuations. I also found that kids in John's special education program were not very different from the inner-city setting, except that they did not belong to gangs. John quickly became acquainted with drug-using friends. Actually, the drug-use problem in this rural county was far worse than in the large metropolitan school.

Within a very short time, the school staff decided that John was simply not able to function in a classroom for very long periods of time. It was decided that he should only attend school half days. Every day when John got home from school, he was supposed to sit down with the after-school caregiver and do homework. The irony was that even though he could not sit still in school, the after-school caregivers believed that they could make him do it at home. It was a constant battle, and he was forever being sanctioned for one thing or another. John had a volatile temper, but he had never been violent to others. Mainly, he would scream and curse, trash his own belongings or his room, or do something to injure himself. He would attempt to leave, and the caregivers would call the police to have him picked up as a runaway who might harm himself. At school, the assistant principal tried to have John arrested for "assault with a deadly weapon" because he threw a paper clip across the room in the direction of one of his teachers. The paper clip hit the blackboard but not the teacher.

The assistant principal decided that next year John should not be in a classroom with other children anymore. She was convinced that his behavior was attention seeking. She isolated him by placing him in a room with an aide who was to give him his schoolwork to do. The aide was there to watch him, keep him on track, and assist him if he had questions. He was not allowed to go to the lunchroom anymore or to interact with any of the other students attending the high school. His behavior became more and more bizarre. One minute he would be bouncing off the lockers that were in that room, and the next minute he would be rolling around on the floor crying. It became clear to me that he was "rapid cycling" from manic to depressed, then repeating this cycle, all in a matter of minutes. Still, the psychiatrists never witnessed these episodes and therefore would not diagnose bipolar disorder. At this point, he was on lithium and Ritalin, but it was clear that they were not working well for John.

Eventually, John was expelled from that school. The school administrators felt he was a danger to himself and others. I had him schooled at home by a tutor for the remaining weeks of the school year. The teacher came to our home six hours per week. She was very good with John, and he did make some progress. She was willing to allow him to walk around during their lessons, and he was actually able to get some schoolwork done that way. Still, it was woefully inadequate.

The next year, the local school district had set up a special school program for kids who had not been successful in the usual EBD programs. John's mental health case manager thought that John would be appropriate for this program. They had a psychologist, in addition to the regular teaching staff, who would be there every day and spend time with each of the children daily. Additionally, John's county mental health case manager would be a frequent and regular visitor to the school.

The school psychologist and the county case manager became alarmed one day because John had burned and cut himself. The case manager came to our house and attempted to get my insurance to hospitalize him as injurious to himself. But the insurance company would not authorize it unless John stated that he was going to kill himself or someone else. John no longer felt that way.

A few weeks later, the psychologist became convinced that John was using drugs and was chemically dependent. The psychologist decided to appeal to my insurance company to give him a chemical dependency assessment. They agreed to have him hospitalized for a day or two for a chemical use evaluation. When I brought him there, the hospital staff was convinced he was on something. John denied this, and I was sure that he had not had the recent opportunity to obtain any drugs. Nevertheless, the staff confronted him on this. I am not sure exactly what happened after that, but John became very volatile, and the staff placed him in seclusion, where he went totally out of control and became psychotic. The staff called the psychiatrist from the psychiatric ward to come and deal with him.

The psychiatrist ordered a dose of Haldol, which quickly calmed him down. John spent a great deal of time talking with the psychiatrist. For the first time John admitted to hearing and seeing things. He said that the last medicine he was given made him feel calmer and think more clearly. The psychiatrist called me and explained that John had been admitted to the psychology ward and explained what had happened. The psychiatrist told me that he thought John was in acute mania. I told him that if he thought that was acute he should have seen him during the previous month because I thought the mania was beginning to subside when I brought him in. The psychiatrist told me that he would like to put him on a different medication, similar to Haldol but with less severe side effects. John developed a severe allergic reaction to the first medication they tried but was placed on a different medication in the same atypical antipsychotic drug class. John really did seem much better on this medication, and for the first time I felt there was some hope for the future.

The psychiatrist told me and the rest of the care team that it was clear to him that I had spent considerable time with John trying to reach him and help him to learn proper behavior. It had never mattered before that I had successfully raised three productive children before John. I was always blamed as one of the factors in John's behavior problems. Now that John was able to think more clearly, he was able to reiterate what behaviors were expected of him. The challenge, however, would be that he was nearly 18 years old and had spent the last 10 years developing secondary behaviors in his attempt to cope with his mental illness and psychosis and now needed to eliminate these behaviors. Additionally, because John was so young when the beginning signs of his mental illness emerged, his social and emotional development was halted at a 3- to 4-year-old level. No one had any clear idea about how to help him catch up on his social and emotional development. But at least now we had the diagnosis that I thought would help people understand and stop blaming him and me for the behavior and really begin to help him. I was soon to find out how wrong that assumption was.

During all these years, the stress had been nearly unbearable, and it was affecting my physical health. At the time John was discharged from the hospital, I was admitted to the hospital and had my sixth abdominal surgery. I was discharged from the hospital after three days, and the next day was visited by the county case manager and the psychologist from John's school. They had decided to drop him from the program, and now it was determined he should go to the Alternative Learning Center (ALC) once per week to pick up assignments and then work at home on his own. I knew this would never work. I told them how incredibly unfair this was because he was not even given a chance to learn how to adapt and change since getting on better medications. But they had already made up their minds. He was discharged from the program, and someone else filled his spot just that quickly.

After John left that program, I was able to get him into an inpatient state mental health hospital program. They had a psychiatrist on staff who actually spent time with my son more than once per week. She diagnosed John as schizoaffective bipolar. This program was the best I had seen to date, and John did get a lot out of the program. It was more successful than others were because they incorporated a behavior modification program that gave real incentives for desired behavior but was not so punitive for undesirable behavior. When children exhibited undesirable behavior, they did not lose all the credit they had built up with good behavior but were simply not able to earn merit points for a set period of time. Unfortunately, that program was time limited, and John was discharged back home to me about four months later.

John spent the next three years trying to complete his high school diploma on a new Individualized Education Program (IEP), all while I was attempting to help him further his social and emotional development. With little to no help from the school or county, I pushed and prodded John until he was able to meet the goals set out by the IEP and get his high school diploma by the time he turned 21. Nevertheless, to this day he is barely literate and has few job skills. Currently, his social and emotional development is about that of a 15-year-old, which makes it incredibly difficult. People expect him to act his chronological age. Progress is occurring, but when it is two steps forward and one step backward it is very discouraging. I have been attempting unsuccessfully for the past year to get John in an assisted living situation because I no longer feel he is making progress living with me and I need some relief before my health really fails me.

Source: Contributed by Cindy Ahler

Questions About the Case

1. How are the different responses of John and his older brother to the same drug for the same problem typical?
2. How are the reactions of the neighbors and the pediatrician to the ADHD exhibited by John and his brother predictable? Why do you think school personnel were willing to see John as having ADHD when the pediatrician was not?
3. If you had been John's daycare provider or his teacher in preschool, how would you have attempted to help John?
4. How would you respond to suggestions that John's mother caused her son John to have EBD?
5. What role, if any, do you think teachers had in John's problems?

6. How, if at all, do you see cultural factors as causing or contributing to John's problems?

7. What would lead you to the conclusion that John's problems were primarily a result of biological factors?

8. Imagine that at some point in the story told by John's mother you were John's teacher. What would have been the most important and helpful things you could have done as his teacher?

C A S E

2

Cases on the Problem and Definition of EBD

Sometimes, we see rather clearly how adverse life circumstances can play a part in emotional or behavioral disorders (EBDs). If we can put ourselves in the shoes of a child or youth, we might imagine how difficult it would be to cope with poverty, abuse, neglect, discrimination, failure, or other situations that we would have to overcome.

Terrence

Terrence (Terry) Singleton has been getting high on drugs and alcohol since he was 8 years old. He says that he stole these things from his mother. He went to jail when he was 14, after being convicted of B&E (breaking and entering) and petty theft. At age 17, he attacked two women, and the judge decided he should be tried and sentenced as an adult. So, at age 18, he got an 11-year sentence.

His record—reports of psychologists, social workers, probation officers, and teachers—and what he says himself, all suggest that Terry has always been a troubled youngster. A psychiatrist who evaluated him indicates that he's confused and desperate. He was neglected by his mother, a factory worker who was often away from home. His mother never married Terry's father. She lived with a succession of boyfriends. One of these boyfriends beat Terry regularly. Terry apparently started stealing marijuana and money from his mother when he was still quite young. Sometimes he sold the drugs he stole from her.

Social services knew when he was 7 years old that Terry's mother wasn't taking appropriate care of him, but nothing was done. Terry was apparently left free to roam the neighborhood unsupervised. He'd break into cars and houses. He wasn't properly dressed, and he occasionally slept outdoors. Eventually, social workers had him living with his father's mother, but his grandmother had 11 other people living in her three-bedroom house, including her daughter with intellectual disabilities. The probation officer who visited this home described it as being in a horrible state of disrepair and smelling terrible.

When Terry started school, a psychologist found him to be below average in achievement. About a decade later, when he was 15, Terry was reading and doing math at about the fifth-grade level. Terry was placed in special education in elementary school, and a middle school teacher described him as desperate for friends and having difficulty establishing relationships. His classmates complained about his bad odor, which may have been caused by his bed-wetting. To keep from being teased, he built a partition around his desk to try to keep other kids out.

Source: Rewritten based on McHugh (1987)

Questions About the Case

1. Should Terry's behavior have been disturbing to his community? Would you consider him to have EBD? Why or why not?
2. What would have been the advantages and disadvantages of early intervention in Terry's case? Where do you think Terry's behavior should have been addressed first, and why?
3. What is the best treatment or intervention for young people like Terry?

◆ ◆ ◆

It isn't at all unusual for students with EBD to carry a different label first, particularly "learning disabled." Kate's teacher tells us about how students in her class said to have "learning disabilities" also had severe EBD. Again, as in the case of Terry, we see how life circumstances could contribute to EBD. But we also see how difficult behavior can be episodic in school and how experiences at school can sometimes counterbalance conditions at home.

Kate

Kate Morrissey exhibited a lot of problems: tantrums, screaming, stubbornness, and neediness. She was incredibly bright, but her appearance and behavior put people off so quickly that they almost never took the time to get to know the "real" Kate. They didn't because she was dirty, "smelled like a dog" (according to a fellow student), and was totally unsociable. She always had her nose in a book—at lunch, at recess, and any time there was a break from structured activities in the classroom. Fortunately, the other students in class didn't tease her a lot; they mostly ignored her.

Kate loved to read, but she wasn't a good speller. She hated to write. Sometimes she whined and moped when asked to do things she didn't like, but other times she became belligerent and frightened other students. On more than one occasion Kate screamed at her teacher and pushed her books off the desk. Sometimes, she was defiant, telling her teacher, "I'm not going to do it, and you can't make me!"

Kate was often puzzling to her teacher. It was virtually impossible to get her to do anything she didn't want to do. She typically dug in her heels and simply refused to cooperate. Yet she showed a surprisingly sophisticated sense of humor, sometimes laughing uproariously with her teacher at a cartoon that other students in the class just didn't "get."

Kate's teacher met her parents—more accurately, her mother and her mother's boyfriend. According to the teacher, Kate's mother was a plain-looking woman with a master's degree in social work and was a caseworker for the county social services department. Ms. Morrissey's boyfriend looked a little "rough" and was remarkably odoriferous, according to the teacher, who said that what little he mumbled was virtually inaudible.

Ms. Morrissey expressed some concerns about Kate's friendships, or lack of them. About uncompleted homework, Kate's mother said, "That is Kate's responsibility. She knows what she is supposed to do. If I make suggestions she either acts as if I'm not there or refuses to do it." The teacher told Ms. Morrissey about Kate's body odor, to which Ms. Morrissey replied, "That's her job, too. She knows she is supposed to bathe every night. When I tell her to shower, she usually responds by throwing a tantrum that may last as long as half an hour."

Kate was tight-lipped, even secretive, about her life outside of school. She did reluctantly confide to her teacher that she lived in a trailer home and that lots of times no adult came home until 11:00 p.m. or midnight. Many nights, she was home by herself, except for Sandy, her pet rat, and Rover, her beloved dog. She boasted that she could take care of herself and wasn't afraid, even though she had no nearby neighbors. On nights when nobody else was home, she fixed macaroni and cheese and treated herself to bags of Oreos. She also told her teacher that her house was quite messy, and she seemed humiliated about it. She said things like, "You wouldn't believe what a mess my house is. You wouldn't want to come to my house."

When Kate was caught sneaking her pet rat on the school bus, she wasn't allowed to ride the bus because having animals on the bus was prohibited. So her teacher offered to give Kate and Sandy a ride home. The assistant principal went along. What they found on their home visit was discouraging.

The Morrissey trailer home was down a long, bumpy driveway, nowhere near any other houses. It was old. The front steps sagged, and the broken storm door was hanging from its hinges. The yard looked like the local junkyard and included an old refrigerator that had been used for target practice. Inside, half of the living room was piled from floor to ceiling with trash. There was a spot on the couch just large enough for Kate to sit and watch TV.

The teacher knew that Kate had been assigned a Big Sister through a program at the local university. Ms. Morrissey had told Kate that she couldn't see her Big Sister until the house had been cleaned up. But cleaning up Kate's room, not to mention the rest of the house, was a gargantuan task not likely to be completed by even three people without hours of work. Kate's room was covered with trash. Books were on the floor. All of her clothes were scattered around the room, none at all in her closet. Dog feces were everywhere.

When Kate arrived at school after the home visit, she was very angry. To her teacher's "Hi, Kate!" she said nothing in response. When asked to hand in her work she threw it at the teacher, screamed that she wouldn't do as asked, and started tipping over desks.

Source: Rewritten based on a case from Kauffman, Pullen, Mostert, and Trent (2011)

Questions About the Case

1. Supposing that Kate's teacher had not made a home visit, how do you think she would have understood Kate's behavior differently?
2. Knowing the conditions in Kate's home, do you see her as having EBD? What do you think were the best strategies for the teacher and principal in dealing with Kate's mother?
3. What do you think would have been the best strategies for Kate's teacher to use in her classroom?

Children and youth with EBD usually present problems to many of the people with whom they have contact. Most relevant here are the difficulties they cause teachers and peers at school. All veteran teachers of students with EBD recall incidents in which the pupils defeated their best efforts to instruct or maintain order. In many cases, teachers marvel at the wild antics of their students or the seemingly unsolvable puzzle their behavior presents. And in retrospect, many leading experts are amused by their own naïveté—which sometimes served them well and sometimes was disastrous—in dealing with students who are difficult to manage and teach. Here are descriptions of her early experiences as a teacher of students with EBD written by Pearl Berkowitz, one of the pioneers in the field of special education for disturbed children.

Pearl Berkowitz

If you could look back and focus on my most vivid memory, you might see me, now the teacher in Mrs. Wright's former classroom, futilely hovering over two hyperactive 12-year-old girls who are fighting about which one should use the free half of an easel, while on the other side of this easel, a big, burly, belligerent boy is calmly painting, secure in the knowledge that no one would dare question his right to do so. Standing near the window is a small, thin-faced, pale, remote-looking boy who is staring at the fish tank, apparently just watching the fish swim around. Next to him, another boy is sitting on the rocker tickling himself under the chin with the mink tails he has just cut off the collar of the school secretary's new spring coat. Two children, a boy and a girl, perched on the old dining table, are playing a loud game of checkers, while another boy is silently resting, stretched out atop an old upright piano which I had inveigled into my room. Sporadically, in the midst of this magnificent atmosphere for learning, some child says to another, "Your mother," and the entire class seems to leap together and land in a football pileup on the floor, while I stand helplessly by.

Of course I made many mistakes, but I hope I also learned something from each. Let me share just one of these early mistakes with you. I was doing my weekly planning when a brilliant idea occurred to me. I decided that the greatest contribution I could make that week would be to bring some culture into the lives of those poor, deprived, disturbed children at Bellevue. To start on this enriching experience, I elected to read to them a favorite poem from my own elementary school days, "The Owl and the Pussycat." Imagine my consternation at the chaos I caused when I reached the lines, "What a beautiful pussy you are, you are. What a beautiful pussy you are." The children actually tumbled out of my room with noisy screaming and guffawing. Within minutes, I was left alone in the classroom, bewildered and unaware of what had caused the difficulty. I had a lot to learn.

Source: Berkowitz (1974, pp. 30–31)

Questions About the Case

1. In what way(s) do you see Berkowitz's management of her class as typical of first-year teachers?
2. What are the strengths and weaknesses of Berkowitz's interactions with her students?
3. In what ways do you see specific children in Berkowitz's class as typical or atypical of children identified today as having EBD? How might EBD students be the same or different today compared with those in Berkowitz's class of the 1950s?

The following four brief cases should be considered together. For each, you are to consider whether the child or youth should be considered to have EBD or not to be so classified. In many cases, there is disagreement among observers about whether a student should be identified for special education. You should be able to justify your decision about a particular child or youth.

Barry

Barry has five older siblings, the youngest of whom is 10 years older than he is. He has always been the baby of the family in everyone's eyes, especially his mother's. He is now a rotund third grader whose torpor is remarkable. His obesity, sluggishness, and infantile behavior (e.g., he prefers to play with small stuffed animals) make him a constant and easy target for teasing by his classmates. Since he entered kindergarten,

Barry's mother has brought him to school daily, sat in her car in the parking lot during the entire school day in case he should "need" her at any time, brought his lunch to him and fed him in the hall or in her car, and whisked him home after school. Her life seems absurdly devoted to his safety and comfort yet ironically calculated to impair his psychological and physical growth and development. School officials suspect that Barry was bottle-fed until he was in the second grade, and they know that his diet now primarily consists of junk foods. He has no friends his age, and he will not participate in age-appropriate play in the classroom or on the playground. He is constantly teased by other children because of his weight and infantile behavior.

Darlene

Darlene's mother was a 12-year-old sixth grader when Darlene was conceived. Recently graduated from high school, the mother is now pregnant with her third child. Darlene is a first grader who frequently gets into trouble because she hits or pokes other children, fails to do her work, and disobeys the teacher. Other children are beginning to shy away from her in fear. She is bright-eyed and gregarious with adults, and the casual observer may not suspect that the teacher sees her as a significant problem.

Nate

Nate is an eighth grader with an IQ in the gifted range. Although he is highly intelligent and creative and scores high on standardized achievement tests, his report cards contain only Ds and Fs. All his teachers and the school principal are exasperated with his constant clowning in class, his refusal to complete assignments (and his insistence that sloppy, incomplete work is sufficient), and his frequent macho behavior that gets him into fights with other students. His mother, a divorced former teacher, is at her wit's end with him at home; he is slovenly, refuses to do chores, threatens her and his older sister with physical violence, and was recently caught shoplifting.

Cleo

Cleo is the wispy 16-year-old daughter of a wealthy attorney. Her favorite book is the Bible; she is preoccupied with remaining slender in this life and earning the right to ecstatic happiness forever in the next. Her schoolwork is always perfect, or nearly so. She has only one close friend, a woman in her early 20s who has a history of suicide attempts. Cleo complains constantly of being tired, unable to sleep, and too fat. She is forever dieting and exercising, and she frequently vomits immediately after she eats a normal meal. She offers profuse apologies for any imperfection anyone points out in her behavior or academic performance.

Questions About the Cases

1. Which of these individuals (if any) do you think should be identified for special education as emotionally disturbed, and which (if any) do you think should not be? Why?
2. What kinds of behavior problems should be of greatest concern to teachers?
3. What should trigger identification of a child or youth as having mental health problems? Should all mental health problems result in a student's being identified as needing special education? If so, why? If no, why not?

3

Cases on History and Current Issues

Perspectives on the behavior of children and youth change over time. Such perspectives, however, usually change rather slowly. Often, we are not aware of how perspectives are changing in our own era. Some of the behavior that once was considered highly inappropriate or deviant is now considered unexceptional. Laws change. But community standards, which are really the basis for many laws, also change. You might consider the ways in which our ideas about misbehavior have changed in the past 10 or 50 or 150 years (or any other interval of time) and the ways in which they haven't changed much. You might also consider changes in how we view children's behavior as desirable or undesirable. Just because something changes doesn't mean it has changed for the better or for the worse. Some changes are good for our society and for children; some are not. First, consider a description from a book published in 1839. You might consider the language really dated. But consider the behavior and its management in language that we'd use today.

N. B.

N. B., aged 16, was described to me by his father, who came to consult me in regard to his management, as a boy of singularly unruly and intractable character; selfish, wayward, violent without ground or motive, and liable under the paroxysm of his moodiness to do personal mischief to others; not, however, of a physically bold character. He is of a fair understanding, and exhibits considerable acuteness in sophisticated apologies for his wayward conduct. He has made little progress in any kind of study. His fancy is vivid, supplying him profusely with sarcastic imagery. He has been subjected at different times, and equally without effect, to a firmly mild and to a rigid discipline. In the course of these measures, solitary confinement has been tried; but to this he was impassive. It produced no effect.

He was last in a very good [school] in a town in———, where he drew a knife upon one of the officers of the establishment, while admonishing him; and produced a deep feeling of aversion in the minds of his companions, by the undisguised pleasure which he showed at some bloodshed which took place in this town during the disturbance of 18———.

He has not appeared to be sensually disposed, and he is careful of property. His bodily health is good, and he has never had any cerebral affection. This boy was further described to me as progressively becoming worse in his conduct, and more savagely violent to his relatives. Still I easily discovered that he was unfavorably situated; for his relations appeared to be at once irritable and affectionate; and the total failure of various plans of education was throwing him entirely upon their hands.

As an instance of the miserable pleasure which he took in exciting disgust and pain, I was told, that when 13 years old, he stripped himself naked and exposed himself to his sisters.

Source: Mayo (1839, pp. 68–69)

Questions About the Case

1. What explanations can you offer for N. B.'s behavior?
2. What interventions are available today that were not in N. B.'s era?
3. How would N. B.'s behavior as described in this case be viewed today?

We often do not perceive (or we forget) the personal experience of pain that someone with an emotional or behavioral disorder (EBD) feels. Sheldon Rappaport, a leading figure in the field of learning disabilities, describes some of his painful school-related experiences as a child. His experiences are much like those of many children with EBD.

Sheldon R. Rappaport

That school day had been like all others—bright with the joy of being with children and blurred in a kaleidoscope of activity. But in late afternoon, there was something different in the way Miss. Joseph asked us to take our seats. Her customary calm and warmth were missing. On top of that, she announced that the principal had come to talk to us. My stomach squinched "danger."

The principal, small, grayed, and austere, spoke in her usually clipped fashion about the importance of working hard in school. As her train of thought thundered by, I was aware only of its ominous roar. The meaning of her words did not come into focus until she made the pronouncement: "Those boys and girls who have frittered away their time, and as a consequence will not be promoted to second grade, will stand when I call their names." Then she called my name.

The shock and mortification staggered me, making it difficult to struggle out of my seat and stand beside my desk. Who stood when she called the other names, the faces of those who remained seated, and what further remarks she intoned all blurred into a macabre dance that encircled my shame. Breathing was painful and had, I was sure, a ridiculously loud rasp which was heard by everyone. My legs rebelled at supporting my weight, so my fingers, aching tripods of ice, shared the burden. In contrast to the cold of my numbed face were the hot tears that welled in my eyes and threatened to spill down my cheeks to complete my degradation.

The principal left. Class was over. Amid joyous shouts, children milled through the door that for them was the entrance to summer fun and freedom. Some may have spoken to me, to tease or to console, but I could not hear them. The warm and pretty Miss. Joseph was there, speaking to me, but I could neither hear nor respond. The borders of my mind had constricted like a hand clutching my pain.

Daily I sat staring at a book that would not surrender to me its meaning. In my war with the book, now and again I was victorious over an isolated word, but the endless legion of pages ultimately defeated me. Repeatedly, I looked back over the unfriendly, unyielding rows of print to find a word that I could recognize. In doing so, my failures amassed by the minute, like a swelling mob jeering at me. Finally, the fury rising within me burst from my fists, while from between clenched teeth I silently cursed the head I was pounding. To me, the immutable reality was that my head was bad. It caused my frustration. It sponsored my shame. I knew no alternative but to beat it into becoming a smarter head. That failed, too, adding daily to my feelings of frustration and worthlessness.

Daily terrors were walking the eight blocks to and from school and going into the school yard for recess. Being all flab and clumsiness and wearing thick glasses made me a ready target for any kid who needed to prove his prowess by beating me up. And the number who needed that were legion. Consequently, a rainy day became a reprieve. To awaken to a rainy morning was like an eleventh-hour stay of execution. It meant no recess outdoors. And nobody who wanted to fight. But even better than a rainy morning was being ill. Only then, in my bed, in my room, did I feel really secure. In the fall of third grade I missed 22 days of school. I was confined to bed with rheumatic fever, as I learned from the family doctor when I didn't have the desired wind for distance running while in college. Despite pains which I can still vividly recall, that confinement is the most peaceful of all my childhood memories.

The only outdoor activities I enjoyed were pretend ones. (The woman who lived in the next row house must have been sainted.) To get me out of the house, my mother put on the open porch the piano stool I played with. It became the steering wheel of a huge, powerful truck (you know how loud they are), which I guided flawlessly along endless highways, gaining the admiration of all whom I passed. At other times, I ventured across the street where the vacant lot became a battlefield on which I, clothed in my father's army tunic and overseas cap, performed feats of heroism and distinction for which I received countless medals and accolades. Those fantasized moments of glory apparently nourished my thin strand of self-respect enough to enable it to withstand the daily siege on my pride.

At night, when the cannonade of derision was still and my imperiled pride temporarily safe, I implored God and the Christ, Jesus, to see to it that tomorrow would not hold for me the tortures of today. I offered all possible concessions and deals, but relentlessly the tomorrows of Monday to Friday were no better.

Source: Rappaport (1976, pp. 347–350)

Questions About the Case

1. Could Rappaport's experiences be very similar to those of a student in public schools today? Why or why not?
2. How might school experiences like Rappaport's be affected by today's emphasis on student achievement, test performance, and accountability?
3. Given a student who faces daily terrors like those in Rappaport's account, how can teachers best handle bullying behavior on the part of other students?

There is something timeless about the nature of EBD. Students with these disorders make themselves unpleasant to be around, and their unpleasantness transcends the era in which they live. Art's behavior would be a challenge for any teacher in any era. However, teacher behavior and expectations may need to change to fit changes in knowledge, attitudes, court cases, and rules for intervention in problem behavior.

Art

Art's personal habits were ugly, to say the least. He seemed to be a sponge for dirt, grease, and filth. His language was also foul. Most people would describe him as obnoxious. He wasn't obnoxious all the time, though. Sometimes, he was actually likeable. But most of the time he made people want to stay far from him. It's hard to imagine a more repulsive 12-year-old, and it's no wonder he wound up in the psychiatric hospital where I was a teacher in the school program.

The schoolwork Art handed in was consistent with his behavior. He picked his nose until it bled and wiped the blood and mucus on his papers. He picked his ears and wiped the wax on his papers. He picked his acne and wiped the blood and pus on his papers. He spit on his papers and smeared the saliva over his answers to try to erase them. When he did use an eraser, he made holes in the paper. He wrote answers in the wrong places and then circled them and drew arrows, often to another wrong place. He wrote four-letter words and drew lewd pictures and swastikas on his papers. He punched holes in his papers, tore them, wadded them, taped them together, ripped them apart again, and retaped them. And he got angry because he couldn't handle the tape very well; it stuck to his fingers rather than the paper. All the while, he muttered curses—he couldn't do the damned work because it was too babyish or too hard or too stupid or too crazy and "what kind of a stupid goddamned bastard was I to give him such crap?"

Art made himself detestable to everyone. He teased and bullied smaller children unmercifully. He baited teachers and threatened other adults. He seemed to be unable to be either clean or pleasant. He called his former teacher "fuckstick."

I had my first run-in with Art at the beginning of the first day I was his teacher. He sauntered into the classroom, looked at me, and said, "Well, if you're going to be in here, then I'm getting the hell out!" Immediately, he was out the classroom and soon out of the building. I knew I had to get him back to my classroom, even if I had to drag him back. I caught up with him just as he left the building. I thought I'd have to struggle with him physically. However, when I reached out to catch him he stopped, looked at me for a moment, and said, "Well, hell! I guess I might as well go back." He got back to the classroom before I did. He never tried to run away again.

But that wasn't our last confrontation. He didn't like homework. He said that if I gave him homework he'd burn it. I replied matter-of-factly that I didn't think he would, since he wasn't allowed to have matches, and that even if he did burn it I had duplicate assignments to give him. "Well, you son-of-a-bitch, you just wait and see," he said. The next morning when an attendant brought him to my classroom he threw an old chocolate mix can on my desk and sneered, "Here's your goddamned homework!" I opened the can and found it full of ashes.

Source: Rewritten from Patton et al. (1991)

Questions About the Case

1. How might a student like Art fare in general education? How should a general education teacher handle a student like Art?
2. What do you think about the teacher's statement about dragging Art back to class and the teacher's expectation of a physical struggle with Art? In what era do you think this incident occurred? How could a teacher deal with Art given the expectation that teachers not touch students?
3. What do you think the teacher's response should be to the incident described at the end of the case?

4

Cases on Conceptual Models

A biogenic model makes physiological processes the center of attention. It, however, does not rule out all other types of interventions. The assumption is that the youngster's difficulties are of neurological origin and can be treated effectively, at least to some extent, by medications. A biogenic model doesn't discount the importance of other interventions, but it does start with the assumption of a biological problem that requires biological treatment.

Erin

At first, the psychiatrist who saw Erin thought she had attention deficit hyperactivity disorder (ADHD). The psychiatrist thought this because Erin had so much trouble paying attention in class, completing her schoolwork, and getting along with other students. Her first three years of school were disasters. ADHD seemed to be a reasonable diagnosis at first because she was having enormous academic difficulties, and she seemed to have all the classic symptoms. So the first prescription Erin got was for Ritalin. The Ritalin helped her a lot, and she seemed to be doing much better in fourth grade. However, it eventually became apparent that Erin had something else, perhaps in addition to ADHD.

When psychiatrists discovered that Erin was having hallucinations, they hospitalized her. She was having severe headaches, too, so they did some brain imaging to check for brain tumors and other neurological problems, but they could see nothing wrong with her neurologically. So they decided to prescribe an antipsychotic drug. Taking the drug helped Erin be able to go home and go back to school. The psychiatrists know the drug was very important in her treatment, but they also know that Erin was able to function as well as she did only with the help of her family and teachers.

Source: Rewritten from Anonymous (1994)

Questions About the Case

1. What reasons can you give for viewing schizophrenia as a mental illness of biological origin rather than as an emotional or behavioral disorder (EBD) with causes in life circumstances?
2. What early symptoms of mental illness did Erin exhibit, and why might treatment of them with medication have been wise?
3. Besides medication, what other interventions do you think would have been important in Erin's case?

The psychoeducational model attempts to combine concern for functioning in the present with understanding of underlying motivations for behavior. Although other conceptual models do not discount the importance of talking to students, the psychoeducational model sees talking things through with the student as the primary strategy.

Sterling

Sterling was placed in special education for students with EBD when he was 14. His most prominent problems were oppositional behavior (refusing to do what adults asked of him) and saying threatening things. He also had the habit of leaving the classroom without permission and wandering around in the halls, not behavior calculated to make him welcome in school. He seemed to like to argue with teachers and taunt his classmates, especially another student, John, who lacked a lot of social skills. And John often teased Sterling, making the situation all the worse.

One day John came in really upset about something, and the special education teacher had to spend a lot of time getting him to calm down. As usual, Sterling needled John, calling him a "fag." The teacher asked Sterling to sit down, but instead he shoved a desk across the room and walked out of the classroom and began disturbing other students. The staff got him to go to a quiet room where they could talk to him. There, they got Sterling to think about his behavior, why he was doing what he was doing, and how he might behave better.

The special education teacher used what is called a "life space interview" (LSI) to help Sterling understand that he was jealous of the time she spent with John. She got Sterling to understand that the situation in her classroom set him off because circumstances at home (older sister with severe and multiple disabilities, sick mother, absent father) reminded him that he'd had to take on a lot of adult responsibilities. Sterling could act up at school and get away with it. It was a safe environment in which he could do what he sometimes felt like doing at home but couldn't. The teacher also helped Sterling understand that she cared about him and wanted to help him be less disruptive.

As part of the interview, the teacher also drew up a contract with Sterling. The contract stated that if he didn't respond to John's teasing and kept his cool and didn't act out, he could spend some time one-on-one with the teacher.

Source: Rewritten from James and Long (1992)

Questions About the Case

1. If Sterling's maladaptive behavior persists, what options should the teacher consider?
2. In what way(s) did the interview of Sterling connect underlying motivations, present problems, and future problems?
3. In what way(s) did the interviewer use techniques associated with other conceptual models?

An ecological model focuses on the social context of a student's behavior. The student is seen as part of a social system that can be changed to support desirable behavior. Rachel's case demonstrates the multiplicity of factors that need to be taken into account to devise the most effective intervention program.

Rachel

Rachel has autism spectrum disorder (ASD). She's 10 years old and goes to a special self-contained class in a public school. Her ASD is on the severe side of the spectrum. She talks in complete sentences, but her language is also characterized by echolalia— repeating words, phrases, or sentences over and over. Through observation of her interactions with teachers and other students, it's clear that the ecology of the classroom must take at least the following factors into consideration and that each must be carefully controlled or regulated:

- number of students in the group in which she's taught (for Rachel, no more than five)
- individualization of media (e.g., pictures, drawings) materials used in discussions and interactions
- length of lessons (for Rachel, no longer than five minutes)
- variation of lesson topics
- group (choral) responding (for Rachel, frequent choral responses)
- predictability of being asked to respond as an individual (for Rachel, unpredictability)

- rapidity of responding (for Rachel, a fast pace)
- student interactions (for Rachel, frequent interactions)

Source: Rewritten from Kamps et al. (1991)

Questions About the Case

1. What are the aspects of Rachel's social system or context that needed to be altered?
2. How is the ecological approach compatible with a behavioral model?
3. Supposing that altering the social context does little or nothing to change a student's behavior (remember that *nothing always works*), what alternatives would you suggest, and why?

◆ ◆ ◆

The behavioral model focuses on problem behavior and ways to influence the behavior. The basic idea is to use manipulation of the environment, especially what happens just before and what happens just after behavior, to change the way a student behaves.

Steve

Steve is a 12-year-old in a regular education class. He's been identified as having EBD, and his teacher receives regular consultation from a special educator. His attention to academic tasks is poor. He also sometimes is overly aggressive and disruptive, both verbally and physically. An observer working in the class recorded Steve's behavior, finding that he was on task less than 60 percent of the time on average and that his behavior was disruptive about 40 percent of the time (percent of the short intervals that his behavior was observed and recorded).

The teacher and consulting special educator started with the assumption that Steve misbehaved for a variety of reasons, including consequences (what happened just after his behavior) and antecedents (i.e., circumstances or context, such as the teacher's asking Steve to complete an academic task). In Steve's case, the teachers put the focus on antecedents. They decided to give Steve choices of several options for work he really didn't like to do. Any one of the options would be acceptable because all of them led to the same instructional objective. Under these conditions, in which Steve could choose any one of several optional ways of doing the work, observations showed that he was on task about 90 percent of the time and was disruptive only about 10 percent of the time. The teachers had to be creative in thinking up the alternate assignments, but the choice of alternatives seemed to work well with Steve.

Source: Rewritten from Dunlap, Robbins, and Kern (1994)

Questions About the Case

1. Usually, we think of the behavioral approach as emphasizing consequences—rewards for desired behavior, for the most part. What behavior principles does the case of Steve illustrate?
2. How does the case of Steve emphasize the importance of a teacher's relating to the student as a thinking and feeling person, even if the behavioral model is being implemented?
3. What are all the factors that, according to a behavioral approach, influence behavior?

CASE

5

Cases on Biological Factors

Sometimes, the biological basis of deviant behavior seems to be clear. Even so, there may be disagreement about the extent to which a youngster (or adult, for that matter) is cognizant of his or her inappropriate behavior and should be held responsible for his or her actions.

Chad

Chad's mother suspected that her son had schizophrenia long before psychiatrists diagnosed him as having the mental disorder. He had always been somewhat odd, engaging in head-banging as an infant in his crib and, when he was older, rubbing his head on the grass until he was bleeding. He also had some ritualistic behavior, such as knocking on a chair before he could sit down. As a child, he repeated over and over before going to sleep, "I'm not going to die, I'm not going to die. . . . " His mother eventually became terrified that Chad would kill himself.

Chad was a bright student with a high grade point average in elementary school. But he was the classic high school "nerd" who didn't date or play sports. Before going to college, he'd earned enough money from selling computers he'd built from parts he bought online to buy a car. In college, he majored in business and computer science.

However, all did not go well in college. He only managed to stay at college one year. First, he was arrested for drunk and disorderly conduct and possession of marijuana, something totally out of character with his upbringing and prior behavior. But his parents were unaware that he'd become psychotic, not just fallen in with bad friends. He became convinced that his scrotum was abnormally large, although a doctor told him that there was nothing physically wrong. He became convinced that his scrotum was so big that it tipped his pelvis forward, making his back rigid and his head tip back. And he felt that people could tell this, that they were calling him "nerd" and "faggot" behind his back. His friends told him they thought he was crazy.

In April of his freshman year, Chad did tell his father by email that he was getting paranoid. He also imagined that his eyes were always glassy white and that he could see a lot of blood vessels in his eyes. His parents thought he was having an anxiety attack. But he stopped going to classes and ended up with an F, 3 Ds, and a C for his course grades.

When his parents picked him up from college in early May, after classes had ended, Chad was uncommunicative. At home, he stayed in his room nearly all the time, seldom bathed, slept all day, and spent the night on his computer. His mother heard him saying such things as "Shut up!" but he denied he was doing anything other than "messing with" her.

Ten days after coming home from college, Chad told his mother about his scrotum. He started cutting holes in his underwear, taping his scrotum up, and wearing the tightest jockstrap he could find. His mother took him to the family doctor, who assured Chad that there was nothing wrong with his scrotum. He wasn't convinced, so his mother took him to a urologist, who told Chad the same thing. Chad did not believe the urologist either.

Thinking that Chad might be schizophrenic, his mother took him to a psychiatrist, who suggested that Chad had "symptoms of a delusional nature and depressive obsessions" and prescribed Prozac and Zyprexa. However, Chad showed minimal improvement with these drugs, which he did not always take, and he started hallucinating (e.g., yelling at nonexistent "oystermen" to shut up because they were yelling at him). He told his mother that he'd found a plastic surgeon online who would do the necessary operation on him for $4,000.

Chad wondered how he could get the money. He tried printing fake money with his computer, but he threw it away because it looked too phony. Before he robbed the bank, Chad tried to perform the surgery on himself. He stopped because of the blood and the pain. Robbing the bank seemed to him the only way to get the money for the surgery. He wore a black knit cap with eye holes cut in it and put on black gloves. He had no weapon of any kind, but he yelled, "Put your hands up, this is a holdup!" when he entered the bank, about 20 miles from his home.

Now he is in jail and could face life in prison. The local prosecutor has charged him not only with bank robbery but also with counterfeiting (remember, Chad had printed bills with his computer, which even the prosecutor admits were too crude to fool most people). The prosecutor maintains that, although Chad is mentally ill, he knew that what he was doing was wrong. And if a defendant can tell right from wrong, then he should be prosecuted to the full extent of the law.

Source: Based on Carlson (2003)

Questions About the Case

1. How is Chad's behavior consistent with the onset of schizophrenia in childhood and adolescence?
2. How do you think schools could have responded better to Chad's problems?
3. To what extent do you believe that Chad should be held responsible for his behavior? Why?

Biological factors are known to significantly contribute to schizophrenia. There are, however, biological factors in all types of emotional and behavioral disorders, including depression.

Peter

Peter is 14 and was referred by his pediatrician due to nonspecific somatic (bodily) complaints, lethargy, psychomotor retardation, substantial weight gain, and frequent napping following his father's murder. Peter had been close to his father, and his interpersonal and academic functioning declined precipitously following his father's death. He spent hours alone in his room saying that he wished he were dead. He said he was too sad to cry. His family was afraid for his safety. His mother and older brother had been taking antidepressants since Peter's father's death, and both reported that the medication was helpful. The family had a history of depression, alcohol abuse, and anxiety. Given the severity of Peter's symptoms, his thinking of suicide, and other family members' positive response to antidepressants, Peter was started on antidepressant medication as well as cognitive-behavioral therapy.

Source: Kaslow, Morris, and Rehm (1998)

Questions About the Case

1. What biological risk factors are evident in this case?
2. What reasons would you have for suggesting that Peter's problems were reactive to the circumstance, not biological in origin?
3. If you were Peter's teacher, what could you do to help address his problems most effectively?

CASE

6

Cases on Family Factors

Sometimes, we can see risk factors at work in a child's home environment. Problem behavior seems to be passed from one generation to the next, not merely through genetic predispositions or other biological factors such as poor prenatal care but through the deviant behavior of parents. We are tempted to overgeneralize and assume that all misbehavior is a fault of parenting. Sometimes it appears to be, but sometimes it is decidedly not.

Sylvain

Sylvain lives with his mother and older sister. Welfare is his mother's only income. His mother has suffered from depression since age 16, was identified by her peers as both highly aggressive and socially withdrawn in the fourth grade, did poorly in school but finished high school, and is separated from her husband, who was drug dependent and physically abusive.

   Sylvain's mother had anemia and diabetes when she was pregnant with him and had to take medication to stop contractions beginning in the seventh month of her pregnancy. Sylvain was born prematurely, and his umbilical cord was wrapped around his neck. At the age of 4 months, he was diagnosed with asthma. He also has chronic otitis (ear infections) and diarrhea. He has been on medication for hyperactivity since he was a year old. He has temper tantrums, is aggressive, and has a tendency to hurt himself. His mother feels inadequate in dealing with these problems.

Source: Rewritten from Serbin et al. (2002)

Questions About the Case

1. What parent and family factors put Sylvain at risk for the development of a serious emotional or behavioral disorder (EBD)?
2. How would you assess the relative contributions of biological and psychological factors in Sylvain's problems?
3. What supports do you think Sylvain's mother needs if she is to deal with his problems most productively?

Sometimes it is easy to miss problems. We make unwarranted assumptions or are unaware of important information. Sometimes we focus so much on school that we miss what is important outside of the school environment. Jack is a case in point.

Jack

In my many years of teaching, I've had some students who've really gotten my sympathy. I thought I'd seen or heard almost everything until I met Jack, a student in my tenth-grade special education class.

First, you need to know how he came to be referred. Jack was referred for special education at age 15. He was then repeating the ninth grade, and yet he was getting failing grades in most of his classes. The referral said he often came to class in "crisis mode," meaning that he paced back and forth and was clearly in distress. Often, his distress was related to his younger brother, Drew, who was receiving special education for a learning disability. Drew was often sent into the hallway near Jack's classroom when he behaved inappropriately, and Jack then felt compelled to talk with Drew in an effort to keep him from getting into more trouble. If he was not allowed to calm Drew down, then Jack would warn of trouble to come.

Jack also frequently got mixed up in other students' problems and had difficulty not letting those stressful situations affect him in the classroom. Every day when he got to class he wanted to see his guidance counselor or another person because he knew that someone was gossiping about someone else. Jack hadn't had any major outbursts in class, but if his requests weren't granted immediately he became frantic and began cursing to himself.

In trying to redirect his anger or alleviate his worry, the referring teacher said that she would converse with Jack in the hallway nearly every time he came to class. She reported that he was fairly responsive to her "positive attention" but that he usually felt the need to stay in the hallway a little longer or go to guidance following these talks.

This teacher also reported that she and a collaborating special education teacher would allow Jack a little more freedom of movement than the other students in the class. She stated that, for the benefit of the rest of the class, if Jack chose to disengage from the lesson by lying on the sofa and pretending to sleep, then the teachers would respect his choice.

As part of the referral and evaluation process, I completed a review of Jack's school records, where I found some shocking information. In addition to failing the ninth grade during the previous year, he had also not passed the state's standardized literacy tests. In fact, he had not passed *any* of the standardized exams administered by the state in the eighth and ninth grades. Jack's discipline record was also extensive. We were only in the second month of the school year, but Jack had already been in in-school suspension for four days and on out-of-school suspension for four days. The records didn't include any information about his specific offenses, but teachers' reports indicated that Jack had problems with profanity, noncompliance, tardiness, and skipping classes. The records also indicated that he'd been having behavioral problems in school since the fourth grade.

I failed in my attempts to contact Jack's parents, and he continued to be suspended from school for various behavioral infractions, some of them resulting in out-of-school suspensions. Finally, a school administrator required one of Jack's parents to accompany him to school for a reentry conference. When Jack's mother came to school with him, the guidance counselor presented her with the form granting permission to evaluate Jack. She signed the form without arguing.

While we were in the process of managing Jack's referral and doing the evaluation, we ran into the winter holiday break. We decided to start Jack's evaluation first thing when we returned to school from the break. When we got back to school, we received some absolutely shocking news. Jack's younger brother, Drew, had been arrested and was being held on murder charges! The story we heard was that Drew and two other teenagers had traveled out of state over the holiday and allegedly attempted to steal money from an elderly man. When the man refused to give them any money, they allegedly overpowered him and strangled him to death with his own shoelaces, then took his money.

Naturally, Jack was tremendously upset by these events. He blamed himself for Drew's trouble and stated that if he'd kept a closer watch on Drew, none of this would ever have happened. We decided to postpone standardized testing, as Jack was too upset for the results to be valid indicators of either his ability or his achievement.

Before long, Jack was in trouble again and was sent to the assistant principal's office. While talking with her, he became very agitated and asked her if she was afraid he was going to strangle her. The assistant principal perceived this as a threat, and Jack was suspended from school indefinitely, pending expulsion.

The school principal told us to proceed with the evaluation right away. However, Jack was not allowed in the school building, so we had to complete our evaluations at the county administrative building. Jack's mother worked two jobs and was rarely home. Jack's stepfather had recently been released from prison, where he had been incarcerated on charges of assault with a deadly weapon. Jack's stepfather was also an alcoholic who'd had his driver's license revoked following several DUIs. So transportation was a major problem for Jack. The school psychologist and I spoke with Jack's stepfather several times on the phone and arranged for Jack to come to the office building to be tested. The school psychologist managed to complete the cognitive evaluation. However, I didn't have such luck. I arranged meetings with Jack's stepdad three times and, all three times, he failed to show up. The school principal wouldn't allow me to go to Jack's home to test him because of the stepfather's history of violent behavior. During this time, Jack placed several phone calls to the assistant principal, begging her to let him come back to school and apologizing for his behavior. He also called several of his teachers just to talk with them.

We finally decided to hold an eligibility meeting without the results of standardized educational achievement testing. The information we did have included a full cognitive and psychological evaluation and sociocultural information, including a great deal of Jack's family history. The psychological data indicated that Jack had average to above-average intelligence, but a considerable amount of anxiety and depression, often manifested by acting-out behaviors.

A social worker went into Jack's home and interviewed his parents. What she discovered was shocking. Jack's mother was not his birth mother. Jack had discovered this when he was in fourth grade—9 years old. He and his brother had been at a local swimming pool one day during the summer when they were 9 and 7, respectively. While at the pool, both boys were approached by a strange woman. She told them that she was their *real* mother. According to bystander accounts at the time, this upset both boys. When they began to argue with the woman, she attempted to hold their heads under the water, seemingly to drown them.

In fact, Jack's adoptive mother confirmed that the woman at the pool was indeed their birth mother and was a former friend of hers. She had no idea who the boy's father was, nor did their birth mother. The man Jack and Drew had believed for years was their real father was, actually, probably not related to them at all.

According to Jack, his home life had been tumultuous. He had a vivid memory of his stepfather attempting to push him out of a moving car when he was a child, and he appeared to be haunted by this memory. According to social services records, Jack's home had been investigated on several occasions by a social worker, but nothing was ever reported to be amiss. Jack's difficulties in school began in the fourth grade and seemed to worsen as he became older. I wondered how so many adults in the schools and in the community could have missed the obvious suffering of a child for so long.

Source: Rewritten from Hallahan and Kauffman (2006)

Questions About the Case

1. If Jack had been identified earlier in school as having significant problems (or a disability), how might subsequent problems have been prevented?
2. How might the teachers and school administrators have responded differently to Jack's insistence on being involved in his younger brother's behavior management?
3. If Jack's family life contributed to his problems at school, what could be done about it? How should his teacher work with him?

◆ ◆ ◆

The family sometimes has a profound effect on a youngster's choices in life, whether the youngster has EBD or not. Of course, having EBD always complicates matters, as the case of Tommy illustrates.

Tommy

Tommy lived in a small apartment with his mother, three brothers, and a sister. He's the oldest child. The family lives on welfare. His mother has a history of years of drug and alcohol abuse and has difficulty holding a job. Tommy and his siblings are basically "raising themselves."

Tommy has been receiving special education services for EBD since he was in sixth grade. At first, he was placed in a self-contained class for students with EBD. When he was in ninth grade, he was placed in the district's alternative school for students with EBD because he continued to have behavior problems. At 18, Tommy has been in and out of trouble with the law for minor offenses (e.g., petty theft). He's been suspended from school several times for things like smoking marijuana in the boy's bathroom, cursing the principal, and fighting with other students. He reads at the early fourth-grade level and has only very basic math skills. Tommy has been taught various self-management and conflict resolution strategies for dealing with his aggression, but none of the strategies seems to be very successful.

Now Tommy hates coming to school. In fact, he has skipped school on many days, hanging out with an uncle who works at an Automobile Service Center. His uncle has worked on cars at the Service Center for over 10 years. Recently, his uncle has been teaching him more and more "tricks of the trade." Tommy is fairly good with cars, and when he skips school to be at the Service Center his social and behavioral skills appear to be normal.

One day, the manager of the Service Center offered Tommy a job as an assistant. The manager pointed out that if Tommy was successful he might eventually have the opportunity to be a mechanic, although the pay would be low in the beginning. Tommy decided to drop out of school and go to work at the Service Center. It's only been a year, but Tommy is doing very well in his new job. His uncle continues to mentor him. However, in order to become a mechanic, he will need a high school diploma and then need to take classes at the community college. Presently, he is working on his GED.

Source: Rewritten from Stichter, Conroy, and Kauffman (2008)

Questions About the Case

1. What family factors may have contributed to Tommy's learning and behavior problems?
2. Was Tommy's decision to drop out of school a smart choice?
3. Do you think he would have better employment opportunities if he had remained in the alternative school until he was 22 years old?
4. Do you think Tommy will be able to continue in a positive direction? What obstacles might he have?

7

Cases on School Factors

The intense, small-group, individualized instruction that should be a hallmark of special education classes is lost when classes are too large. Even the best of teachers can be swamped by excessive demands. It is also true, however, that some teachers make bad choices of what and how to teach students with special needs. Students may not receive the special instruction they should in a special class or resource room for a variety of reasons, as the following teacher's account illustrates. Do not be fooled into thinking that an emotional or behavioral disorder (EBD) does not exist among students labeled *intellectually disabled* or *developmentally delayed* or some other special education category. Students with any label may exhibit highly problematic behavior, and many students in special education have multiple disabilities.

Jeremy

I haven't always enjoyed teaching children with special needs. There have been some years when my aid[e] and I closely perused the "help wanted" section of the newspaper every afternoon after the kids left. We decided that cleaning houses, digging ditches, or washing windows from a scaffold would be less tiring and more lucrative than teaching.

We were never as stressed as we were the year Jeremy came. In the spring, all of the special classes for children with mild mental retardation were full (i.e., at or over the state limit). Some of us pleaded with administrators to open a new class for the fall. If preceding years were any indication, the system would declare a number of children in the system eligible for services after the year started. And there were always eligible students who moved into our area. But less money was available than in previous years, so salary for a new special education teacher was not in the budget.

Predictably, a new student, Jeremy, moved to our system from another state. Our supervisor asked the superintendent to sign another waiver for him to be placed in my class. He did, and Jeremy came. My class limit was 12. Jeremy was number 17.

Jeremy's educational plan was troubling. Even though he was a third grader, with an IQ score well above some of my other students, all the academic areas were categorized as "pre-readiness." Even my kindergarten students were ahead of Jeremy academically! It was clear from the information in the psychological folder that Jeremy would probably be lost in even my most delayed academic group and would require individual attention for academics.

I was fortunate to have a talented and skillful student teacher that year who took over some of my other groups so that I could devote several blocks of time to Jeremy. He soon let me know that he did not appreciate the effort! Even though I had tried to be *very* reinforcing of *any* effort on his part, he clearly was not going to go quietly to the academic trough. He whined, cried, screamed, and usually refused to participate in any instruction. I allowed him to make as many choices as possible during every lesson, reduced the length of the lessons, and increased the reinforcement. But his resistance increased. He also added verbal aggression toward me. When his mother came to observe a lesson (at my insistence), she said, "Well, *of course* he's unhappy. You're making him *do things*!"

The things I insisted he do were to trace his first name, to match four letters of the alphabet, to count objects (no more than 10). I had determined from the IEP what skills he had, planned highly structured lessons with lots of built-in choices for him, and rewarded him with objects *he* had requested (stickers, free time, stars on his papers). And he got meaner every day!

I asked his mother for a description of Jeremy's day at his previous school. There had been *no* small group or individual instruction, only whole-class instruction. His day started by finding the day on the calendar, determining the day's weather, and stating what was appropriate to wear. "They sang a lot of songs that were academically reinforcing, such as the alphabet song. Jeremy knows a *lot* of songs." Jeremy's mother had volunteered regularly in this class and was impressed with the amount of art work the children did. Every day they spent at least an hour or more (never less) on art, a half-hour exercising (even though they also had a [general education] gym class), and had a safety lesson.

"Mrs. Wheatley, Jeremy's teacher, also showed a lot of wonderful films and slides," she said. She went on to tell me all about the films and the picture books that the children could look at afterwards.

When I asked if Jeremy was writing on lined paper in his former school, she said, "They weren't ready to write yet."

I was angry. Here was a third-grade child with an IQ of 65 who had not participated in any mainstreaming program (his class went everywhere *en masse* and separately) and had had little or no academic instruction. It wasn't that I disapproved of Mrs. Wheatley's projects. I taught the calendar, sang songs, did art, and discussed safety. I also thought it important that the children learn to write their names!

Usually, my aid[e], student teacher, and I switched groups often so that I could keep an eye on *all* my students. When Jeremy came, I was not as flexible. I didn't want to ask those with less training to handle a *very* difficult child. But soon, the behavior problems in the other groups made themselves known. I had 17 children and five reading groups, and it soon became apparent that I needed a half hour somewhere for *another* reading group. My aid[e] voiced my opinion: "Pat, we got too many individuals to individualize." Indeed!

Source: Kauffman and Pullen (1996, pp. 3–4)

Questions About the Case

1. How do special education teachers come to avoid effective instruction of the students in their classes?
2. What should a teacher do when class size limits or other legal or administrative requirements are waived?
3. In what specific ways did the schools and classes Jeremy attended contribute to his misbehavior?

We must consider how disordered emotions and behavior look and feel from the perspective of the child or youth. Our conceptualizations cannot be complete until we have been able to set aside the analysis of *problem* or *disorder* from the adult's perspective and see it through the child's eyes. In popular contemporary literature, we find many examples of the child's perspective. Consider, however, one example of the youngster's view of school-related problems taken from the personal retrospectives of a noted special educator who worked with students who have serious problems. This special educator clearly experienced serious and painful problems of adjustment in childhood, but she was not identified as mentally ill or in need of special education.

Esther P. Rothman

From the start, I hated school, deeply, irrevocably, and silently. Kindergarten was an anathema. Rather than take me to the doctor every other day with sore throats and stomachaches that were strictly school-induced, my mother finally capitulated and let me stay at home. First grade was no better, however, and as my sore "threats" would no longer work, and as the compulsory school laws prevented my mother from withdrawing me, I had no alternative but to start off for school daily and then divert myself to the rocks and crevices that then underlay the Hellsgate Bridge in the new and growing suburb of Queens, twenty minutes away by subway from the lower East Side where I was born.

I wonder if teachers really appreciate how overwhelmingly frightening it is to be a truant. Fear possessed me completely—fear of ridicule by school-loving seat-mates, each of whom was smarter than ten of me put together; fear of God, who was certainly going to punish me by striking my parents dead; but, most of all, fear of tongue-lashings by arm-twisting teachers, who were going to debase me by "leaving me back." Which indeed they did. I was a "holdover." My teacher didn't bother to explain to my mother why I was left back, but she clearly told everyone else. I couldn't read. And I couldn't read because I played hooky—or so she said. The fact that I was already reading Hebrew and the exotic adventures of Dickie Dare in my friend Lilly's third-grade reader was totally unknown to my teacher, yet I am certain, even now, that if she had known it, she would not have altered her decision.

My teacher was what I knew she was—anti-Semitic—because my mother told me so. This was a word I learned very early in life, and I accepted it casually as I accepted being an alien, one of only four Jewish children in the entire school. I felt special—not a bad feeling, but not completely good either.

I was never permitted to hold the American flag in front of the class for our morning class salute—a sacrosanct ceremony in every classroom in the entire school. My shoes were never clean enough. Once I was told I had lice. Or sometimes I did not have a handkerchief safety-pinned to the lower shoulder of my dress; this handkerchief always had to be in that exact same spot—never elsewhere. I never figured out how it was that we were supposed to blow our noses, and I never asked. I settled it myself. I had a handkerchief for showing and a handkerchief for blowing. And usually I forgot one or the other or both deliberately because I firmly believed that good little girls should never need to blow their noses at all. It was too crass. Instead, I stuffed pencil tip erasers up my nostrils. As for boys, I never even wondered what they did. Handkerchiefs were not within their generic classification.

These memories come flooding over me as I write—the hurt of being labeled a liar by a seventh-grade teacher who did not believe I had written a composition using the word *chaos* because I could not give him a definition of it. Did he never understand that I knew the word *chaos* down to my very toes because I felt it deeply every day of my life in school? Then there was the day my fifth-grade teacher threw into the garbage can the chocolate cake my mother had baked for a class party and which the children had voted to give to the teacher because it was the prettiest cake of all. And going farther back, I remember staring at the school map that hung—large, frightening, and overwhelming—from the border of the chalkboard and trying desperately to find New York State while not another child spoke—every eye, especially the teacher's, was glued to me. But worst of all was the indignity, fear, and humiliation of having to cheat on a test because I could not remember whether four-fifths equaled 80 percent.

Source: Rothman (1974, pp. 221–222)

Questions About the Case

1. What experiences described by Rothman might be similar to those of children in school today?
2. How can teachers make certain that they know what their students can actually do?
3. How can teachers make certain that they do not discriminate against children because of their ethnic or cultural characteristics?

Surprises are part of teaching children with EBDs, even after one has been at it for many years and become highly skilled. Mistakes and disappointments, as well as successes and gratification, are part of the territory. A special education teacher describes an unexpected response to a good teaching procedure with Barry, a 9-year-old youngster who exhibited a variety of problem behaviors, including failure to play appropriately with other students.

Barry

A consultant suggested that I try to provide positive reinforcement for Barry when he was behaving appropriately. So I tried to do this, and I thought I was being successful. But I had one particularly frustrating experience in following the consultant's suggestions. Let me tell you what happened.

I was working one day with another group of children in a different part of the room. From across the room I saw that Barry was playing quietly and appropriately with another student. I saw my chance to use positive reinforcement for his doing something good, so I hurried over to him, knelt down beside him, hugged him, and said, "Barry, I really like the way you're playing quietly with the blocks and having fun with Susie." He jumped up, gave me a strange look, and yelled at me, "Well, fuck you, shitload!"

Source: Rewritten from Patton, Blackbourn, Kauffman, and Brown (1991)

Questions About the Case

1. What was the teacher trying to do in this case? Was she using an appropriate strategy?
2. If you were advising this teacher, would you suggest that she continue her attempts to improve Barry's behavior or abandon them and try something else? Why?
3. What do you see as the central problem in this case (e.g., Barry's play behavior, Barry's language, the teacher's attempt to improve Barry's behavior)?

◆ ◆ ◆

When a teacher has success with a student whose disordered emotions and behavior have presented major problems, the gratification is enormous. Consider the sense of accomplishment the teacher must have felt in the following case.

Andy

Andy started in my class on Valentine's Day. He was no Valentine. He didn't think teacher directions (e.g., "It's time to line up for lunch") were very important. When Andy wanted to play in the free-time area, he expected to be allowed to do so, and he protested loudly when he wasn't. In short, Andy wanted to do what he wanted to do when he wanted to do it without any interference from anyone, including teachers. He reminded me of a line from a Bogart movie: "I want what I want when I want it." Andy soon found out that I was not Lauren Bacall.

His teacher from the previous school in another system called me after he had been at school for two days. She was loaded with information about his family and academic information not included in the psychological folder, such as cues to give him to stop some of his undesirable behavior.

I also made a home visit. Andy's mother, Mrs. Johnson, received me in her immaculately clean dining area. She never looked at the IEP changes I wished to make in Andy's educational plan. She never looked at me. She looked at the razor strap on the table. This strap had been cut in two, had a leather thong in the top which she pulled onto her wrist. Twice, while I was there, she banged the strap on the table when one of the children was too loud or too close for her comfort. Mrs. Johnson signed the addendum to the IEP, and I left. I also vowed that Andy would get *lots* more attention from me, my aide, the principal, the speech pathologist, and anybody else I could strong-arm into doing a favor for me.

It was imperative that we get Andy in his seat, get him to stay in his seat, and to complete work that his previous teacher assured me he could do. He was fascinated with the box of shells I had collected at the beach the previous summer. I sorted them into sizes and promised him one of the tiny shells for every problem he worked correctly. I had bags and bags of shells at home that had cost me nothing, and he loved them. Soon he asked, "Instead of all those little shells, how about if I get a bigger one for a whole sheet?" We discussed that the papers had to be neat, mostly correct, as well as completed. He thought that was fair. My aide found an old pencil box, covered it, and helped him glue his shells onto the box—a treasure chest. In the meantime, I sent him with good notes all over the school; to the principal, the guidance counselor, the secretary, and anybody else who expressed an interest in Andy.

Andy's work habits improved. His behavior improved. And, after a while, he began to give his shells to the younger children in the class, or back to me at the end of the day. It wasn't long before a sticker on his paper displayed on the bulletin board was enough for him.

Instead of going to the guidance counselor, principal, or secretary for stickers for his papers, he began to give his good papers to them, happy for their praise and their thanks.

The following year, he needed much less reinforcement. It seemed he was proud just to finish a paper. "I do good work, don't I?"

Source: Kauffman and Pullen (1996)

Questions About the Case

1. What are the advantages and disadvantages of talking to other teachers about one of your students and reading the student's records before you start working with him or her?
2. What are the advantages and disadvantages of making home visits?
3. What do you see as the primary indications that the teacher was successful with Andy?

8

Cases on Cultural Factors

Culture can contribute to the problems of children and youth in a variety of ways. Ordinarily, we think of culture as peculiar to a particular ethnic group. Culture, however, is a much broader concept than the behavior or traditions of a group identified by its ethnicity or national origins.

Teri Leigh

Teri Leigh had been removed from her home when social workers discovered that her mother's boyfriend was sexually abusing her. She and her two little brothers had been placed in separate foster homes. Her school records indicate that she has both learning disabilities and emotional disorders. She has, in fact, been diagnosed as psychotic, but I have not seen any behavior suggesting that she is having visual hallucinations or hearing voices. She is very imaginative, but I have no way of knowing whether some of the things she's reported are actually true. She is generally well behaved, but she seeks affection like a much younger child. Her affection-seeking behavior seems out of character for a 12-year-old, especially because she has a grown-up appearance for her age.

Several weeks ago, I taught the basic lesson on pregnancy and childbirth in family life class. A couple of days later, other girls in the class told me that Teri Leigh was claiming to be pregnant. I noticed that she had started bringing baby clothes to school, and there was a lot of secretive talk among Teri Leigh and the other girls. Eventually, Teri Leigh told me she thought she was pregnant. I asked her why she thought so. She explained matter-of-factly that she was probably pregnant because of what her mother's boyfriend had done to her. I explained to her several times that this was impossible because what he had done happened so long ago, but she refused to believe me.

Then I found out that Teri Leigh had given several nude photographs of herself to two high school boys who ride her bus. Luckily for us, the boys gave the pictures directly to the bus driver, who gave them to the principal, Bob Farris. When Bob called Teri Leigh's foster mother, Mrs. Overton, she told him that the pictures had been taken by Teri Leigh's foster sisters. Mrs. Overton claims that she told the girls to tear up the pictures; obviously, they had not obeyed. She refused to discuss the matter with Teri Leigh. She said that is my responsibility. Bob Farris agreed with her. So I made a stab at it.

One day I kept Teri Leigh after school and talked with her for a long time. I told her about how much I love my kids but how much time they take from me, how I have very little time for myself. I also talked to her about AIDS and other sexually transmitted diseases. Unfortunately, Teri Leigh insisted that she wants to get pregnant. And she also insisted, in spite of all the facts I gave her, that she would eventually get pregnant because of her experiences with her mother's boyfriend. I was completely unable to get through to her. What do I do now? I want to help her, but I don't know what to do next.

Source: Rewritten from Kauffman, Hallahan, Mostert, Trent, and Nuttycombe (1993)

Questions About the Case

1. How might biological, family, school, and cultural influences have contributed to Teri Leigh's behavior?
2. What should Teri Leigh's teacher do next? To whom should she turn for help?
3. What cultural factors make it particularly hard to address the problems of children like Teri Leigh effectively?

Sometimes a school, a community, or a society can be considered as a case. Many people who work with individuals with problems or disabilities are concerned about the commitment of our society to those in need. Contemporary antitax movements severely limit the funds available to address the problems of children and families.

The Health and Welfare of Children: How Important Are They in American Culture?

The Children's Defense Fund periodically reports statistics attesting to the plight of America's children, particularly those at greatest risk. In the mid-1980s, the fund's report suggested that a large percentage of American children were living in poverty and that few citizens seemed to care. In 1995, demographer Harold Hodgkinson addressed this same issue, also noting how little Americans seem to care about children. Indeed, in the first decades of the 21st century, nothing much seems to have changed, and many lawmakers in state and federal governments express the opinion that expenditures for programs and services for poor families and their children must be cut dramatically. Hodgkinson's critique raises questions about American culture that remain relevant today:

> Who really cares about America's poor children? An astonishingly small percentage of the U.S. adult population, apparently. Looking at the demographics, we might see some reasons. Only a minority of families have a child of school age.

We could guess that many adults have no daily contact with a child under age 18. As the median age of Americans rises and children become a smaller percentage of the population, things get worse for kids. People are really self-interested and vote for their immediate self-interests. As fewer adults have contact with children in their daily lives, there's going to be even less political support for programs benefiting poor children, most of whom live in central cities and rural areas. But most adults live in suburbs.

People who describe themselves as "pro-life" or "pro-choice" don't express much concern for the children who have *already* been born. Adults pay scant attention to news reports of poverty among this nation's youth. Given the lack of interest in the problems of poor children, any action to address the poverty of America's young people seems highly unlikely.

Source: Rewritten from Hodgkinson (1995)

Questions About the Case

1. To what extent is it advantageous, and to whom, to fund government programs for the poor at low levels so that tax rates can be kept low?
2. If services for poor children are not funded by government, what are the alternatives? What does unwillingness to provide *public* funds for social service programs say about a culture?
3. To what extent can government officials be convinced to fund social service programs that require substantial expenditures in the near term but save money in the long term?

Sometimes we do not have the courage to intervene in the misbehavior we see, partly because of our fear of being culturally insensitive and partly because we live in a culture in which much troublesome behavior is tolerated or ignored. Put yourself in the position of the writer of the following case and think about what you would have done—or what you think someone else should have done.

What Would You Have Done?

As soon as we got to the mall, I knew it was a mistake. I loved taking my 3-year-old there on quiet weekday afternoons, where we could stroll the mall in peace and quiet, toss a few coins in the fountain, and end up in the food court for two kid-sized smoothies. We almost never went at night, and never on a Friday night—and now I knew why. The place was packed, and I could barely maneuver the stroller through the mass of people. The crowd was a surprise, but more disconcerting to us both was the noise level and the rowdiness, both of which were due to throngs of teens roaming the mall, many in groups of eight or ten or more. There was laughter and horseplay, but I was surprised at the roughness of their behavior—pushing and shoving each other, often into other shoppers—and language; there was no attempt at all to conceal their frequent use of profanity and extremely coarse language, especially about members of the opposite sex. There were plenty of adults around, but everyone seemed to be ignoring these kids and their behavior.

One group had me quite unnerved, as they seemed to notice my son and me in particular; they gestured directly toward us at the food court, and seemed to be cracking jokes about the baby stroller or the stuffed animal my son held. I could not fully hear everything they said—except that the profanity was clear. What bothered me even more about this group in particular was their age—I imagined they were not more than 12 or 13 years old, and at least one in the group looked to be no older than 10. There were four boys and two girls.

Overwhelmed by the crowd, I decided to cut the evening short, and made a U-turn toward the parking lot. As I did one of the members of this group called directly toward me—to my son, really—saying, "Hey, little man, let me see your elephant." I can't describe the emotions that ran through me at that moment, and in fact I'm not quite sure what I felt. I know I was shocked they were speaking to us, but also angry, and probably just a little frightened that there could actually be some danger here beyond my 3-year-old being exposed to a lot of profanity and behavior I'd rather not have him see. I had just heard these teens talking graphically about sexual encounters, tossing racial slurs (their group included African Americans, Caucasians, and one Asian teen), and homophobic taunts to each other and even to total strangers. And now they were talking to my 3-year-old.

My gut told me to ignore them, but as we had to pass right by them to get to the parking lot, I decided to let them know I didn't appreciate their behavior in front of my child. A confrontation was more than I wanted, however, so I put on my best teacher-face and merely gave the young man who had spoken the sternest look I could muster. To my surprise and dismay, however, he looked me right in the eye and shot back almost immediately, "What the [expletive] are you looking at, [expletive]?" I'm sure they all saw the stunned look on my face, as I really didn't know what to do or say. Of course I wanted to tear into this young man, asking who he thought he was to talk to me or my son or anyone that way. But I did my best to ignore his question, and wheeled right past them and out the door toward my car. They all hooted as we passed them by. It was a good distance across the dark parking lot to my car, and I really wished I could spot the elderly security guard we had talked to on our way in earlier. But I just pushed the stroller onward, felt for my keys in my coat pocket, and hoped like heck those teens hadn't just followed us out the door.

Questions About the Case

1. In what historical period do you suppose this case could have taken place? Why?
2. If you had been the narrator, how would you have resolved the situation with the youth? If you had been a bystander, what would you have done?

3. Do all students face different behavioral expectations inside and outside of the classrooms? If so, how might the discrepancies in expectation affect student behavior?
4. How does the event in this case illustrate the difficulty in distinguishing antisocial and violent behavior that demonstrates disability from such behavior that demonstrates criminality?

CASE

9

Cases on Attention and Activity Disorders

Attention deficit hyperactivity disorder (ADHD) is one of the most common diagnoses of childhood, and it affects mostly boys. Often, ADHD is the diagnosis given before another, usually more serious diagnosis. And ADHD often occurs along with (i.e., is comorbid with) the diagnosis of another disorder, such as depression, conduct disorder, or schizophrenia.

Loren

At age 7, Loren had one of the worst cases of ADHD the clinician who made the diagnoses had seen in nearly 30 years of practice. He was continuously in motion and had horrid outbursts of temper and other bad behavior at home and at school. He frightened his older sister, at least once threatening her with a knife. He destroyed property in his rages. He had fights with his parents, who frequently had to pick him up at school. He really needed medication, and Ritalin did help him some when he was a youngster. However, his behavior didn't improve significantly, so the psychiatrists he saw increased the dose to very high levels (70 milligrams/day; the usual dose is 20–30 milligrams) and added two antidepressant medications to his prescription.

After he was dismissed from a day camp because of his outrageously obstreperous behavior, a doctor suggested adding an antipsychotic drug. Loren appeared to have not only ADHD but to be depressed and have a conduct disorder as well. Loren's parents were fed up with medications and took him to a different psychiatrist who took him off medication and used more traditional talk psychotherapy. He also started going to a private special middle school for students with problems like his, as his mother didn't think he'd be successful in a regular public middle school. Loren became better behaved and started relating to well-behaved peers in the neighborhood.

Then, a big turning point came when Loren was in the private middle school. He got a dog from his grandparents. The dog apparently gave Loren something to look forward to every day. When the dog his grandparents gave him died (it was already old when Loren got it), Loren's parents got him another dog, with the understanding that he'd have to pay for its care. In the process of setting boundaries for the dog by setting up an invisible fence, Loren got a job with the invisible fence company, which led him to meet dog trainers and to become a trainer himself. In late adolescence, Loren enrolled in a dog training school, where older classmates treated him with respect and didn't refer to his disorder.

Loren went on to found his own company, an obedience school for dogs. He also has five dogs of his own, which seem to keep him calm.

Source: Rewritten from Seiss (2011)

Questions About the Case

1. In what way or ways is Loren's case typical or atypical of children with ADHD?
2. What role do you think the special school played in the eventual outcome for Loren?
3. Do you think Loren should have been prescribed medication for his problems? Why or why not? Do you think his medication was managed properly?

A very common misconception is that children with ADHD (or similar diagnoses of attention and behavior problems) are being overmedicated, that minor problems typically lead to the prescription of drugs, that children are often given drugs for questionable reasons, that too many parents and teachers simply want a mindless conformity or uniformity that drugs produce, that drugs like Ritalin are typically ineffective, and so on. The truth, however, seems to be quite the opposite of these popular notions (see Warner, 2010). Danny is a case in point.

Danny

Danny's mother had ADHD. Hers wasn't diagnosed, though, until Danny started showing the same behavior or symptoms she'd shown. She'd been ridiculed by her peers, teachers, and some of her family members because she lacked organizational skills, was verbally impulsive, and had difficulty concentrating. People thought these were signs of laziness and passive-aggressive tendencies. But in spite of the criticism of others, which carried significant social and emotional costs, she learned to live with the burden of it and became a successful professional.

But when Danny started having similar difficulties she opposed putting him on medication. She assumed that psychotherapy would resolve the problems or that the problems were caused by the pressures of modern urban life, the lack of outlets for Danny's physical energy, and food substances (the chemicals in fast foods, for instance). But, eventually, she decided to try medication. She started to realize that the idealized world involving family, food, school, and so on, just wasn't a realistic expectation. She realized that her son's professional ambitions would be sacrificed if he flunked classes, forgot or lost his assignments, and so on. So, although she could see alternatives, Danny's mother realized that medication, if it worked, would be the best route to take.

For a while, Danny's family sent him to a private school, but this required them to live in cramped, substandard housing, work overtime, forego vacations and meals out so that they could pay the tuition. Danny suffered with this plan, too.

Now Danny's mother and he are doing much better because he's taking a low dose of medication that works. She still wishes she could do better for him, but in a regular public school he's passing his courses and getting through most days without being ridiculed and bullied. Danny's mother is concerned about the possible side effects of the drug, but at least Danny, who is intellectually superior, is doing well in school.

Source: Based on Warner (2010)

Questions About the Case

1. What are options other than drugs, such as Ritalin, for dealing with attention problems?
2. Why do parents resist giving their children drugs for ADHD?
3. What are the side effects of drugs for ADHD, and how worried should parents be about them?

Attention problems, including the diagnosis of ADHD, often occur with other disorders. Sometimes an ADHD diagnosis comes first, followed by another. But often the other doesn't replace the ADHD label; it is added on. Thus, we might find ADHD, followed by conduct disorder (CD), schizophrenia, autism spectrum disorder (ASD, which can include severe autism or a milder form called Asperger's Syndrome), or some other designation that can supplant or be added to the observation that the child or youth was first observed to have significant attention problems.

Rupert

Rupert has Asperger's Syndrome (AS) in addition to serious attention problems that inhibit his ability to learn and get along in life generally. For example, he might pick up a ringing phone and speak into the hearing part rather than the mouthpiece or hold a cell phone with speaking and hearing parts reversed, not paying enough attention to realize his mistake.

None of the usual drugs prescribed for ADHD have improved Rupert's behavior. A psychiatrist suggested Risperdal (risperidone), a drug usually prescribed for serious emotional/behavioral problems like schizophrenia and bipolar disorder. It is said also to reduce irritability and temper outbursts, which Rupert does not have. But Rupert's parents have decided, after reading a newspaper article critical of the use of Risperdal, not to give Rupert the drug.

Fortunately, Rupert attends a special school geared to his needs. So he does okay in school. However, although he is comfortable in this school and relating well to other students with special needs, his attention problems are not being addressed with appropriate medication. Rupert's father is worried that his attention problems haven't been addressed adequately. In fact, for years he's worried more about Rupert's attention difficulties than anything else. Furthermore, he is concerned that after he (himself) dies, Rupert will be preyed upon by others.

Source: Based on Warner (2010)

Questions About the Case

1. Were you Rupert's parent, what would you worry most about? Why?
2. How might a school program give appropriate attention to a student's attention problems?
3. In what ways might attention problems make an individual especially vulnerable to being preyed upon?

Having a student with ADHD can be very difficult, but helping the student learn academic and social tasks can be very rewarding. It is one thing to deal with students in the abstract or consider cases that involve others, but quite another to interact with an actual child. Here, the teacher who provided a personal reflection for the textbook interviews a student with ADHD.

Cleo Holloway Interviews Marvin

Ms. Holloway:	Marvin, what has been your experience at school?
Marvin:	Okay, but it could have been better.
Ms. H:	Why do you think it could have been better?
M:	Because of my behavior. When somebody says something to me, I just take off. I have a quick temper.
Ms. H:	What is the most difficult task for you?
M:	Managing my temper.
Ms. H:	What do you normally do when your temper goes off?
M:	I get mad. I be ready to fight. I don't want nobody to say nothing to me. I want everybody to get along.
Ms. H:	At this point, do you see yourself as successful in school?
M:	Sometimes. I try, but sometimes I end up messing up.

Ms. H:	How would we know when you're about to have a bad day?
M:	I talk back. Get smart. Blurt out. Act up.
Ms. H:	What kinds of things can we do to make you more successful in school?
M:	When I get mad, you can have me be by myself or let me help y'all.
Ms. H:	What do you think you need the most help in?
M:	Controlling my temper. The medicine don't help.
Ms. H:	When do you take your medicine?
M:	In the morning when I first come to school. And it take about 30 minutes to start working.
Ms. H:	If you don't take your medicine, what happens?
M:	I can be bad without it, and I can be good without it.
Ms. H:	Is there anything we can do about managing your behavior and getting your work done?
M:	Not about my behavior.
Ms. H:	Can you get your work done?
M:	I try. Sometimes.
Ms. H:	Name some behaviors that you do that you know keep you from having a good day.
M:	Fighting, skip class. When I get here in the morning, I go to the cafeteria and take my medicine. Then I'm supposed to go to class, but I don't. When I go to class, I make jokes and people laugh.
Ms. H:	How does it make you feel when people laugh at your jokes?
M:	I be breaking up and liking it. I start rankin' on my friends.
Ms. H:	And this is during instructional time, right?
M:	Yeah. [Marvin expresses dislike for teachers and describes getting into a fight in the neighborhood before school, then resuming the fight at school and being physically restrained by a counselor.]
Ms. H:	When you came in yesterday morning, none of us knew what had happened in the neighborhood. We didn't know you had a fight, and we were trying to keep you in school. And that's what we want to do because we know you're very bright. I know you have a hard time ignoring people who are saying things to you, and you feel you have to defend yourself, but how is that going to help you in school if you play into that kind of stuff every single day?

M:	I didn't want to fight, but I couldn't back down because he hit me first. I know kids shouldn't fight, but sometimes you have to. But I could ignore it. But if he hits me, I'll hit him back.
Ms. H:	Can you ignore him, then?
M:	I can. All I gotta do is walk away.
Ms. H:	What types of goals do you have for yourself?
M:	Get out of this bad class. I don't care who knows I'm in the bad class.
Ms. H:	How can you get out of classes that are labeled? What do you need to do?
M:	Do my work. Stay out of trouble. Get to school on time every day. Stop ranking.
Ms. H:	Yes, stop ranking. That's a big one. 'Cause you like to rank.
M:	Yeah, I be doing stuff too, but I ain't gonna blame it all on me. It could be teachers quick to say, "Oh, he's got problems, don't pay him no mind." They're quick to say that. Or, "He's a problem child. You know, he didn't take his meds yet." You know, teachers try to put me down.
Ms. H:	We need to encourage you so you can get your work done. . . . If you think about your life five years from now, in five years you'll be . . .
M:	In college. I'll be 18 and on my way to college.
Ms. H:	So what do you want to be or do then?
M:	I want to be a cop.

Questions About the Case

1. If you were interviewing Marvin, what questions would you ask?
2. In what way are Marvin's responses typical, and in what way are they atypical, of students with ADHD?
3. Would you judge Marvin's aspiration to become a policeman realistic or unrealistic? Why? How would you talk to Marvin about becoming a cop?

CASE

10 Cases on Conduct Disorders

Blame is easy to find in cases of conduct disorder (CD). These are children who try the patience of their parents and teachers, often bringing out the worst in adults. Between episodes of their disorder, however, they may give the appearance of being quite normal or typical, and their interactions with peers and adults may during these times be quite desirable.

Don

Don was 6 and a half, a slender boy about four feet tall. However, he looked sort of sleazy. He looked sort of like a postcard that's spent too much time in someone's hip pocket. He was slouched in a chair in the reception room of our clinic.

I found out that his violent temper outbursts frightened people. They seemed to be triggered by relatively minor provocations or even routine demands, like the teacher's asking him to turn in his homework, someone's giving him a mild rebuke, or an adult's suggestion that he had made a mistake. Such things could lead to his shouting obscenities, overturning desks, or attacking another student. People who observed him at home commented that he ruled whatever territory he occupied. When he was not home, you could depend on it that his progress through the neighborhood could be tracked by phone calls reporting his misdeeds, like his leaving school two hours early, stealing candy from a nearby store, and taking a neighbor child's toy.

Don's parents had difficulty finding a babysitter who would put up with his behavior, so his parents had long ago given up the idea of having a private life, going out to movies, or having weekends together. Both of Don's parents worked. His mother, an attractive woman in her late 20s, looked as if she had a severe illness. The family doctor prescribed medication for her chronic depression and accompanying fatigue. For her, work was a respite from her morning and afternoon conflicts with Don. Her day usually began at 7:00 in the morning, when she had to get him up. He'd usually wet the bed, and she changed the sheets. Then she'd scold him until he went sullenly to the bathtub. Once he was in the tub, she washed him. Then, when he got out, she dried him as if he were an infant or visiting royalty.

Dressing was a task at which Don usually dawdled, and his mother typically gave him a steady stream of prompts and commands to try to get him to speed up.

He typically refused his mother's suggestions about what to put on, and this often led to bitter exchanges ending with his mother's exasperation. Don emphasized their disagreements by kicking the door and throwing things around the room. All the time, his mother hovered around him, helping him get dressed, alternately cajoling, scolding, wheedling, and glaring at him.

When Don ate, his mother stood in attendance. She not only served him, but eventually fed him whenever he was willing to open his mouth. Throughout mealtime, there were yells, cries, and arguments about whether his mother had any right to make him do anything he considered unreasonable. Observers noted that Don's mother alternated between patience with and antagonism to his arguments and threats. One time at breakfast she brought a stick out from a hiding place, and it seemed clear that she often used it. Facing the threat of the stick, Don temporarily complied with his mother and very slowly got ready for school.

When he came home from school in the afternoon, Don picked up the conflict where he left off in the morning. He used his 4-year-old brother, a skillful manipulator in his own right, as a partner. His little brother knew just when to probe, when to attack, and when to withdraw crying and run to the protection of his parents. For example, as Don sat eating ice cream (with his fingers), his little brother slyly got a spoon into the mess and ran triumphantly down the hall to hide behind the door in his bedroom. Don ran after him shrieking. When he got to the bedroom he grabbed the door and slammed it repeatedly into his younger brother. The screams of the 4-year-old got the attention of both parents, who rushed to the scene. Don's father listened for a moment to the shouted claims and counterclaims of both boys, but soon began to slap both of them. Don's mother watched briefly, then walked quietly back to the kitchen and sat staring out the window.

Later that day the family was to go for a ride. Both parents began shouting commands. In the heat of the moment, they often gave contrary or confusing, simultaneous instructions. For example, the mother demanded, "Don, wash your face right now," while the father ordered, "Put on your jacket, Don. Hurry up now." They gave a steady stream of commands as they moved toward the car. The boys took their time and mostly ignored both parents.

Observers noted that during the day there were periods where the interactions of the family members seemed warm and positive. For example, on numerous occasions one of the parents read to the boys, and the boys would often sit for long periods of time seemingly entranced by the story. At times like these, they seemed to be the prototypical loving family.

Source: Rewritten from Patterson (1982)

Questions About the Case

1. Why is it easy to assume that parents do not really love their children with CD?
2. What sets children with CD apart from their peers without this disorder?
3. What suggestions would you have for parents and teachers of children like Don?

Knowing what is the best educational environment for students whose behavior is extremely aversive to others is not simple. It demands thinking about what is best not just for the student whose conduct is unacceptable but for other students as well.

Albert

When I observed Albert just before Christmas in the resource room where he was taught one-on-one, he was noncompliant with reasonable requests (e.g., "Sit in your chair"), and verbally and physically aggressive toward his full-time aid[e], his teacher, and his classmates on the playground. He had frequent tantrums, vomited and ate his vomitus, blew his nose and wiped the mucus on others.

Albert had not started his academic life isolated in the resource room. When his parents registered him at school, they requested that Albert be fully included in the general education classroom. And even though the psychological folder from a school in another state delineated Albert's difficult behaviors, the strong medications he took every day, and his institutionalization for three months the previous year, the school agreed to the parents' request. They placed him in a second-grade class. Albert was a rising third grader, but was so small that parents and school administrators decided that he would do better in the second grade.

I was consulting in this school, and as part of this process I interviewed the teachers who were responsible for Albert's education. Mrs. Tinsley, the second-grade teacher, had volunteered to have Albert as part of her class. She had special education training, had fully included other children with disabilities successfully in her class, and was looking forward to Albert's coming. Her second-grade class consisted of "mostly well-behaved achieving students." Albert was coming to the Dream Team— to experienced teachers who wanted him and to classmates who would be good role models for him.

But Albert had not read the textbooks. He continued the unpleasant behaviors mentioned in the psychological folder; wiping mucus on others when his will was thwarted, screaming constantly, vomiting (once into the printer because he didn't wish to stop using the computer), pulling and grabbing the other children's clothes, biting adults for no apparent reason other than that they were there. At first, according to Mrs. Tinsley, the other students wanted to help him. They became "big brother" or "big sister" to him. Most of the interactions his classmates initiated with him consisted of trying to cue him to comply with teacher requests, and praising him on the rare occasions when he did—just what we would have taught them to do as peer confederates.

Although a few students encouraged him to misbehave, most wanted to help him. After a while, according to Mrs. Tinsley, the students were afraid and confused by Albert's behavior. School personnel could not find strong enough rewards (or effective response cost procedures) to moderate Albert's behavior. He continued to vomit and eat it, to yell and scream. Even though all the teachers involved with Albert tried to cue him about appropriate and inappropriate comments, he still initiated conversations with classmates by asking them if they loved him or if they would marry him.

He continued to pull and to grab the other children's clothing and tried to urinate on the boys when he went to the bathroom.

Albert was gradually isolated more and more in the resource room with his full-time aide. Since most of the resource students were taught in the general education classroom, Albert and his aid[e] had the room to themselves much of the day. Even then, life was difficult, and many of the aberrant behaviors remained; the tantrums, the biting, the vomiting, and wiping his mucus on others. He added pinching to his repertoire of tortures. Albert became a despotic dictator who engaged in any and all of the aggressive behaviors mentioned if he did not get his way. The aide and teacher maintained a program of strict rules with sanctions for not complying and rewards for obeying. Gradually, the aid[e] and teacher began to see moderate improvements in Albert's behavior. Although most of his problem behaviors did not totally disappear, Albert did establish a relationship with both the aid[e] and the resource teacher and began to improve academically and behaviorally. Even then, he tested them periodically. The resource teacher remarked, "Just when I feel like I have a handle on this little boy, he proves me wrong."

Source: Kauffman and Pullen (1996)

Questions About the Case

1. How would you describe the environment that would be least restrictive for a child like Albert?
2. When should a student's classmates' welfare be weighed in choosing an educational placement?
3. If you were Albert's teacher, what strategies for reducing his noxious behaviors would you try?

◆ ◆ ◆

Children and youth with CD are not usually very nice to other people—at least not when they are exhibiting the behavior that gets them labeled as having CD. They, however, usually do not kill people. But there are exceptions, like Larry.

Larry

Mystery, age 9, and his older brother Larry, age 12, often got into fights with other kids in the neighborhood. One time they were observed beating an autistic child on the neighborhood playground. But in spite of such incidents, Mystery was well liked by neighbors and was said to be a happy child.

Mystery's older brother Larry, however, was another matter. Neighbors said he liked sports and video games and had a girlfriend, but he also got into frequent fights, hit people in the face with sticks, and said to them, "I'm crazy. Don't mess with me." He often wore masks to hide his face. According to neighbors, he would walk around the area with his face covered by a bandanna and a book cover over his head to make it look as if he had horns.

Mystery and his mother were bludgeoned to death by Larry, apparently with a metal bar. The 12-year-old did not have an arrest record, nor was there any documented history of his abuse, and the police have been able to identify no motive for the crime. The mother was said to be devoted to her children. She was a single mom and held two jobs to support her family. Larry is scheduled for a psychiatric evaluation in the youth facility where he is being held.

Source: Based on Klein and Harris (2006)

Questions About the Case

1. Why do you suppose no one took Larry's behavior prior to the murder as a serious matter of concern—serious enough to do much about it?
2. Given his history of antisocial behavior, Larry clearly could be considered to have CD, but what other emotional or behavioral disorders (EBDs) do you think might have been involved in this case?
3. What do you think are the primary reasons that most people identify problems like Larry's only after a dramatic, often tragic incident?

Children with covert antisocial behavior often exhibit overt antisocial behavior as well. In fact, multiple problems are more the norm than are isolated problems. George is a case in point.

George

George's first-grade teacher, Mrs. Anderson, came to the child study meeting concerned about his behavior, which was frightening her and her other students. George was highly noncompliant, aggressive, and abusive to himself and others. Some teachers thought George should have a full evaluation immediately, but an administrator demanded prereferral strategies in Mrs. Anderson's class. Mrs. Anderson was visibly upset, even though she was given a list of strategies recommended by "experts."

Mrs. Anderson faithfully followed the strategies and documented the results for two weeks. George was no better. She described George's daily fights with his classmates. She also told the child study committee how George had stolen a tooth from another child's backpack in an attempt to get a reward from the "tooth fairy." After he was told that if he lost one of his own teeth he would get the reward, but not if he stole someone else's tooth, George put a block in his mouth, chomped hard on it, broke his tooth, and demanded a reward. The school nurse corroborated the story.

The administrator who had demanded prereferral strategies maintained that the female teachers were overreacting, that George was just a normal, active little boy.

However, George's fighting, cursing, and stealing increased in spite of the best efforts of the teachers. In fact, his behavior got worse. Mrs. Anderson refused to plead his case before the child study committee anymore. "What does it take to get you people to refer a student? Murder? Suicide?"

George stomped the innards out of a dead bird one day on the playground. He cackled and laughed while stomping. He hit a teacher who tried to stop him from throwing rocks at other kids on the playground. And his teacher told others that one day he stroked her breast and said, "This'll be our secret. Don't tell anyone, and we can do it again."

The final act that got George referred was hanging from a railing around open steps to the basement level of the school. Had he lost his grip, he likely would have been very seriously injured or killed. He was finally referred, found eligible for special education, and placed in a special class for students with emotional disturbance. The class was on the second floor of the school, and George made repeated attempts to jump out of the window. After being moved to another school with only one floor, he tried repeatedly to run away, and his violence escalated.

Source: Rewritten from Kauffman and Pullen (1996)

Questions About the Case

1. What might have been done to prevent George's increasingly troublesome behavior?
2. If George were your student, what would be your primary objective? Why?
3. What suggestions would you have given Mrs. Anderson for prereferral interventions?

◆ ◆ ◆

Children and youth who steal, lie, or exhibit other covert antisocial behavior may carry a variety of labels. They may be considered as having intellectual disabilities, learning disabilities, or giftedness. The common thread among them is their sneaky, unacceptable behavior that puts them at odds with others, both their peers and adults in roles of authority.

Timothy

Timothy began his second-grade year in my class for students with mild mental retardation (intellectual disabilities). He was tall for his age (8). His smile, complete with dimples, was heart-melting, and he had large brown eyes. I thought that he was one of the most physically appealing children I had ever taught. He also learned quickly—too quickly for a child with cognitive problems, and after a few months I insisted that he be reevaluated.

At first, the support teachers, the librarian, the music teacher, and the physical education teacher, all thought he was a precious child. Or, as the librarian said,

"Precious and precocious." However, the honeymoon was short-lived, and Timothy began to torment the students in my class and those in general education. Mr. Allan, the gym teacher, escorted him back to my room one day and said, "The other children in the class have been complaining about Timothy always picking on them, but until today, I never caught him at it. Here's the bent paper clip that he's been sticking children with." He handed me a paper clip that was redesigned to hurt.

When I informed the instructional assistant that Timothy had found a paper clip and used it as a weapon in gym, she said, "Patty, we're missing almost a whole box of paper clips. Maybe we'd better ask Timothy if he can find them."

Timothy politely complied when we asked him to empty his backpack on the table, but protested loudly when about 30 paper clips hit the table. "Somebody put those in my backpack. I swear to God, I never took your paper clips!"

Later, my aide said, "There are other supplies missing, Patty. We'd better watch him."

That afternoon, I visited Timothy's mother, Mrs. Agnor, and asked permission to mark all of Timothy's possessions with a small dot with a magic marker. I also asked her if we could make a list of everything that Timothy had in his backpack every morning, including snacks and lunch. I explained to Timothy and his mother that either the instructional assistant or I would check his desk and backpack several times during the day, and if we found items that did not have a dot on them or were not on the list he would have to return the items and lose some of his free time. Mrs. Agnor asked me to call her immediately if we found any stolen items. I agreed.

For about a week, Timothy had no unmarked or unlisted items, and I was feeling good about the plan his mother and I had implemented. Then one morning I found a fancy pencil, an eraser, and a plastic ring, all of which resembled things from my "treat box" (the box in which I kept things to give my students as rewards or treats for good work). When I asked him where he had gotten those things, he said, "People give me things. Other teachers give me stuff."

My aide and I listed and marked all his items, including the treats.

Several mornings after that, Timothy had prizes that I suspected came from my supply; however, when I discussed this with my aide, we both wondered how Timothy could reach the box of treats, which was on the top shelf of the closet. We had to use a step stool and stand on our tiptoes to reach them. We also wondered when he could steal. Every morning, he participated in the breakfast program, which I supervised, and when he finished breakfast he went to general education for homeroom. According to his homeroom teacher, he was never late.

One morning, a kindergarten student walked into the corner of a table for the third time that week, and when I comforted him he said, "Well, why you all time movin' that ol' table?"

My aide and I realized that the table was a bit off kilter every morning, and both of us had assumed that the custodian had moved the table when he cleaned. But my aide said, "Isn't it puzzling that all of the other tables in this big room are always where we leave them in the afternoon? Seems just that one is always out of place."

When I spoke with Timothy, I gently held his right hand and placed my other hand on his chest. I said, "Timothy, you have been stealing from me, and after we have a talk, I'm going to call your mother. I want all of my treats returned."

"No ma'am, I didn't take those things. How am I gonna get up on the top shelf of that closet? Tell me that!"

"Okay, while we were on duty, you opened the closet door, pulled the table over to the closet, stood on the table, took what you wanted, put the box back, and then dragged the table back."

He looked scared, and I thought for a moment that he was going to cry. "I'm sorry. I won't steal from you again."

A few days later, a new student registered in my class. Brian was a handful, and on his second day in my class he threw an eraser at another student and hit him in the back of the head. I asked Brian to accompany me into the hall so that we could have a private chat. On the way out the door, Timothy murmured, "Man, don't let her touch your chest. Just don't let her touch your chest."

That's when my aide and I realized that Timothy was in awe of my right hand, which he assumed had the power to discern lies and read minds. We never told him otherwise.

Source: Based on an interview with teacher Patricia Pullen

Questions About the Case

1. In what ways did Ms. Pullen follow acceptable or suggested procedures for dealing with youngsters who steal?
2. Supposing that Ms. Pullen had not been able to figure out how Timothy was stealing, what would have been the consequences or outcome for Timothy?
3. What alternative ways of confronting Timothy about his stealing could you suggest?

Covert antisocial behavior includes such things as breaking and entering and fire-setting. Such acts frighten most adults in the areas in which they occur as well as the peers of the miscreants.

Olin and Ricky

Olin and Ricky, both 13, have been charged with setting fire to three houses, doing half a million dollars in damage, and with breaking and entering. Two families had to be relocated because of the fires. Nobody was injured, thanks in part to another 13-year-old, Megan, who noticed smoke coming from a house and alerted the occupants. The police have not identified any motive for the crimes.

Megan said it was scary to watch the fires, and she also said it's shocking that someone her age would set fire to houses. Neighbors are stunned that children would do such things. One of the adults in the neighborhood said, "How can I go on vacation when something like this could happen?" The neighborhood is considered safe, the families in the neighborhood are friendly, and youngsters are nearly always riding bikes or playing basketball in the cul-de-sac in which the crimes occurred.

Both Olin and Ricky are being held in a juvenile detention center.

Source: Based on Somashekhar (2007)

Questions About the Case

1. What would be possible motives for acts like those of Olin and Ricky?
2. How would you suggest trying to prevent behavior like that exhibited by Olin and Ricky?
3. What responses of adults, including parents and legal authorities, and peers would probably make antisocial behavior like that of Olin and Ricky more likely?

Students with CDs can seem very threatening in the abstract, and sometimes they are. However, all of them are individuals who must be treated with respect and kindness by teachers who help them learn academic and social skills. Ms. Njoroge is the teacher who provided a personal reflection for the chapter on CDs in the textbook. Here, she interviews one of her students.

Ms. Njoroge Interviews Marko

Ms. Njoroge:	Tell me about the Linden Center.
Marko:	Do you want me to say what I tell other people?
Ms. N:	Just describe what kind of a school it is.
M:	It's like a probation school; everyone that got in trouble is in this school. It's a school for kids that are messed up and are all in one place. It's a little school with a bunch of rules. You get help with the things you need there.
Ms. N:	Is there anything you'd like to add?
M:	It's a cool school, too.
Ms. N:	What are some of the things you liked about attending school there?
M:	I liked that everyone accepted everyone. No one was judged by their appearance, everyone knew that everyone had problems there and was cool to each other. There was a lot less fighting and drama between people. The teachers were more caring at the Linden Center; in public schools the teachers didn't really care. The teachers were more sincere about what they said.
Ms. N:	I'm a little afraid to ask, but . . . what were some of the things you didn't like?

M: Ha-ha-ha. I didn't like Leave the Groups.

Ms. N: No one will know what that means; so what didn't you like about the Leave the Groups?

M: I felt at times we were being treated as children, and in public schools you can get away with a lot more.

Ms. N: Could you be more specific?

M: We couldn't mention anything sexual or gang-related, which you could get away with in a public school. I also would get bored being in one class for the whole day. I didn't like eating in my classroom either. There was no place for the kids to get together and socialize, like a patio.

Ms. N: What are the things the school has helped you with in terms of behavior?

M: I learned to take cool-outs instead of acting on my anger.

Ms. N: What are some ways you have changed in the past six years, since being at the school?

M: I don't gangbang anymore and I have calmed down a lot. I'm not into fighting as much anymore. I've learned to not be like that.

Ms. N: What do you mean?

M: I don't want that future anymore, because there is too much stress when I am always getting in trouble. I also want to set a good example for my little cousin.

Ms. N: What helped make this change?

M: At school I learned how to talk out my problems rather than fight and also to resolve conflicts. I learned you could be mad at someone and work it out.

Ms. N: Even though I already know, what are some of the things you feel you do well?

M: I rap very well, I have a quick mind; and I can come up with lyrics really quick. I am what you say, musically inclined.

Ms. N: What does that mean to you?

M: That means anything to do with music I am good at. This includes making beats, writing lyrics, everything.

Ms. N: Other than music, are there other things you are good at?

M: I am easy to get along with.

Ms. N: What are some of the things you struggle with or are currently struggling with?

M: I am having trouble getting along with my mom and am also having trouble finding employment.

Ms. N:	Are the two related?
M:	No, with my mom we just don't click. We argue about everything and she trips on me about basically everything. In terms of getting a job, the problem is I've applied to a bunch of jobs, followed up, and get nothing. I think it's because of the way I look with my shaved head and my style of clothes.
Ms. N:	What do you see as obstacles to your success in the future?
M:	I think that in the music industry it is going to take a lot of things to prove myself. I will have trouble doing that because I am going to have to be patient and I am going to have to get to know how the industry works, do things that no one else is doing and step up to the plate in terms of competition.
Ms. N:	Do you foresee any other difficulties you may encounter down the road?
M:	Other than music I will probably have problems with money. I don't see myself having a stable life or living with consistent money. It will take a long time for me to make any money, which may cause me to have more stress with my mom.
Ms. N:	Do you foresee any problems in your education or academically at junior college or trade school?
M:	Academically I don't see any problems in a music school because this is what I like, this is want I want to do.
Ms. N:	How will you handle the obstacles you mentioned, such as being patient and getting along with your mom?
M:	I will keep my mind busy so that I don't focus on my frustrations, like hanging out with my friends and going to parties.
Ms. N:	What about your mom?
M:	I'll have to move out; I think for the first few months to a year it will be tough living on my own and being responsible for bills. I think that once I get the hang of it, it will be all right, though.
Ms. N:	Is there anything else you want to add?
M:	No, that's it.

Questions About the Case

1. What are the advantages and disadvantages of a school like the Linden Center for students like Marko?
2. How would you talk to Marko, were you his teacher, about his past and future?
3. What advice, if any, would you give Marko about relating to his mother?

11

Cases on Special Problems of Adolescence

These three brief cases should be considered together.

V. K.

V. K., a teenager serving a 15-year sentence for the second-degree murder of a 16-year-old classmate, will not have her sentence reduced. She was a 15-year-old senior when she became involved in a knife fight with another student at a school bus stop. Testimony in her trial indicated that dozens of students and adults stood by without intervening as the two fought. The girl who was stabbed bled to death from a wound in her neck, one of several she received in the fight.

Scarface

The child, nicknamed Scarface because of the cuts and scars on his face, was 10 years old, only five feet tall, and weighed just 90 pounds. He was accused of molesting a 10-year-old girl on school grounds while one of his friends held her down. The judge released him into the custody of his parents. Over the next 10 weeks, he was arrested five more times—more times than any other juvenile in Washington, DC, in that year. His other arrests were for holding up and robbing two men, threatening a woman with an iron pipe, participating in a brawl, illegally entering a car, and assaulting a woman and stealing her purse.

Sammy

Sammy was identified as eligible for special education services when he was in the first grade. In addition to qualifying for services under the category of emotional and behavioral disorders (EBDs), he was found to have mild-to-moderate mental retardation (now known as intellectual disabilities). When Sammy was 15, he was picked up by the police at 10:00 p.m. for questioning regarding a burglary at a local clothing store. After an hour of questioning without his parents or an attorney, Sammy indicated that he knew something about a killing at a convenience store in town earlier that year. Sammy waived his right to an attorney and proceeded with the interrogation without notifying his parents. He eventually confessed to being the triggerman in the shooting. Although the details of his story did not fit the facts of the case, Sammy was tried as an adult and, based on his own confession, convicted and sentenced to more than 50 years in prison. The irony in this case is that Sammy was considered to be unable to meet the standards for a high school diploma in the state of Virginia (based on a series of minimum competency tests), but he was considered competent to understand the decision to waive his rights to an attorney during his interrogation.

Source: Based on newspaper reports and personal experiences

Questions About the Cases

1. Should any of these students be considered adults in the justice system?
2. Under what conditions would you not hold people legally responsible for their behavior?
3. Under what circumstances would you consider onlookers who did not become involved or participants equally as guilty as the individual who did a criminal or antisocial act?

The problems of adolescents often involve acting-out behavior, better known as conduct disorder (CD). Often, acting out in school is accompanied by or followed by other serious problems involving delinquency, sexual behavior, or substance abuse.

Matt

Matt is a student in a seventh-grade modified self-contained class for students with EBD. He's included in a regular homeroom and goes to lunch with his age peers in general education. In his homeroom, he often jumps onto a desk and stands on it. When a teacher asks him to get down, he usually leaps from desk to desk shouting, "You can't catch me!" He's then likely to fling himself on a student who's standing nearby.

Matt seems to get into a lot of trouble. On one occasion he wired his homeroom's overhead projector so that when others touched the metal casing they got shocked. Another student told on him, so this never happened to the teacher and nobody got hurt.

Once, Matt tore down the entire ceiling of the restroom. He has destroyed ceramic fixtures and started fires in the restroom. He now has to be escorted to and from the restroom by an aide. His inability to handle unstructured time in his homeroom and unsupervised activities elsewhere in the school is a contrast to his successes in the highly structured special class. There, in the special class, he seems to be under much better control.

Source: Rewritten from Kauffman, Lloyd, Baker, and Riedel (1995)

Questions About the Case

1. How would you describe the prognosis for a student like Matt?
2. Were you advising his teachers (both special and general educators), what suggestions would you offer?
3. How would you respond to someone's suggestion that Matt needs to be with his general education peers so that he can learn appropriate behavior?

◆ ◆ ◆

We too often forget than many adolescents make it through difficult times, that they are resilient in ways that many of us can hardly imagine. Corwin (1997) provides richly descriptive, fascinating stories of how adolescents in environments that exposed them to gangs, delinquent behavior, substance abuse, and early sexual experience were able to resist many of these negative pressures. We have written our own descriptions of some of the young people he depicts in his excellent book. In some ways and at some times, nearly all adolescents exhibit problem behavior. In many instances, they overcome the negative influences of their environments or are able to correct their problem behavior. Teachers, both general and special, may be positive influences on adolescents' behavior.

Latisha

Latisha demonstrates her excellent writing in an AP English class, but her oral language is that of impoverished East Los Angeles, a kind of "ghettoese." She wears her hair in dyed-blond cornrows. She tells her teacher that reading James Joyce's *Portrait of the Artist as a Young Man* was heartrending for her, as it reminded her a lot of her own messed-up family. She has been struggling with her own history.

She grew up in a housing project with her mother, brother, and her mother's boyfriend. She attended elementary school in Huntsville with mostly middle-class white students. She was not part of the gifted program until she was allowed to take a special IQ test and, to the amazement of her teacher, made it into the gifted program.

Reading Joyce prompted her to recall her sexual abuse by her mother's boyfriend, starting when she was 8 and continuing until she was in the fourth grade. Due to the sexual abuse, she became angry, hostile, and withdrawn, started fights with other children, and let her grades slip.

Although Latisha's mother broke up with her boyfriend when Latisha was in the fourth grade, thus ending the sexual abuse, her mother then began using crack cocaine and left Latisha and her brother alone for days at a time. When her mother was home, she physically abused Latisha, who started wearing long-sleeved shirts to school to cover her injuries. When she was in the eighth grade, relatives sent her to live with her father in Los Angeles because they considered it safer for her. Her father had no room for her, so she lived with an aunt, who put her to work cleaning her house and babysitting.

In high school, Latisha was lonely and started drinking, often bringing gin and juice to school in the morning. She was an alcoholic at the age of 15. Her early sexual abuse haunts her.

Source: Based on Corwin (1997)

Willie

Willie is six feet four inches tall. He has a full beard and a diamond earring. He gives the impression of being in his mid-20s, but he is just a large and gifted high school senior. He is a popular student who has been active in student government since ninth grade and is taking several honors classes.

In an essay written for an AP English class, he reveals much that his teacher did not know. His family was stable until it was destroyed by his mother's drug (crack cocaine) dependency. He watched her go to prison. His father, a Vietnam vet who worked for the postal service, encouraged him to be successful in school and never missed a parent-teacher conference. His friends envy his relationship with his father. But Willie often felt alone, abandoned by everyone.

Willie's mother was released from jail, but immediately went back on drugs. He saw her on the front lawn, disheveled and disoriented. Seeing her this way made him cry, as he loved and missed his mother.

After considering going to Pepperdine University (near Los Angeles) on a scholarship, he decided, much to the dismay of his father, to attend Morehouse College in Atlanta. Eventually, his father approved of his decision.

In their high school, Willie was elected homecoming king and Latisha was homecoming queen. Few of the students who elected them knew what these two students had lived through.

Source: Based on Corwin (1997)

Questions About the Case

1. Why is it that Latisha became an alcoholic, but Willie did not become a substance abuser?
2. Had you been Latisha's or Willie's teacher in elementary school, what could you have done to help improve their lives?
3. Supposing you had been Latisha's or Willie's high school AP English teacher, what are the things you could have done to help them most?

Michele Brigham contributed the personal reflections feature for the chapter on special problems of adolescence in the textbook. Here, she interviews three students she was teaching.

Michele Brigham Interviews Carrie, Kate, and Larry (Individual Interviews, Different Responses)

Ms. Brigham: If there was one thing you could change about school, what would it be?

Carrie: The group situation. I don't like how people are classified into different groups. You've got the Goths, the preps, the rednecks. I don't like that. I think everybody should get along. . . . You see a lot of them hang out, and you still classify them into different groups.

Ms. B.: If there was anything you could change about yourself to make school easier, what would you change?

C: I don't really think I'd actually change anything about myself. I know I have an attitude problem, and I'm working on that. But I don't think I'd change anything. Because I don't think my schooling is about me. It's my attitude, and that's just about it, and I'm working on that one.

Ms. B.: If you actually made that change, how do you think it would affect you outside of school, after you're done with school?

C: I think it would help me a whole lot if I changed my attitude, because I sometimes open my mouth about things that I really shouldn't. And I think it'd make life a little bit more easier for me.

Ms. B.: What do you think you want to be doing when you get out of school?

C: I definitely want to go to college. I either want to go and be a lawyer or a doctor. I like the whole doctor scene. I want to do something with helping people. I definitely want to do that. I'm a hands-on person helping people. I definitely want to do something like that.

Ms. B.: Is there anything in school that's helping you toward that goal?

C: Well, not at this point, but next year I'm taking a nurses class over at [the vocational-technical school] that'll give me a little feel for what I'm doing, what I'm getting into.

Ms. B.: Is there anything in school that's keeping you from that goal?

C: Not to my knowledge. No.

Ms. B.:	Have you ever thought about dropping out?
C:	No. I've told my father it doesn't matter how many years I'm in high school, I'm going to graduate.
Kate:	No. Not ever.
Larry:	Well, I'm 18 now. I became 18 last month. Pretty much no. But one of my teachers gave me the idea that maybe I could, because I'm 18, drop out and get a GED [general equivalency diploma] and completely skip my senior year and go straight to college. And I thought about that, and I asked some people, and everyone seems to agree that it's a bad idea.
Ms. B.:	And you're comfortable with that?
L:	Yeah. I'm a year older than I should be because I got held back in first grade. Because I was a little hoodlum back then. Caused a lot of trouble. And I really wish that hadn't happened because I won't have many friends next year. Because almost all of my friends are seniors.
Ms. B.:	What's made you decide to stay in school?
C:	I have a boyfriend now who didn't finish school, and he regrets it. And my father and mother dropped out of school, too. And they regret it to this day. And they tell me, "You need to finish school," but I've always promised my grandparents and everyone I'm going to make something of myself, and I am. I don't care how many years it takes me just to graduate high school, I'm going to make something of myself.
K:	I don't know. It's just my goal to graduate and be with my brother. He's the only one to graduate [from high school] from my biological family.
Ms. B.:	Think about the way you want to be five years from now. Is there anything about yourself you want to work on to get to that goal?
C:	I want to work on accepting me for who I am. I really have a bad problem with doing that. Whether it's like in choir and I can't sing or, like, it's beauty pageants I go to and I don't win or something, I need to accept myself for who I am, because I really can't change myself. Wish I could, but it'd be a little silly I think. But I need to work on that.
K:	Have a better attitude about things. I seem to get mad if I don't understand something. They say I have attention disorder or something.
Ms. B.:	When you get mad, what problems does that cause you?
K:	I get frustrated and just want to stop doing whatever it is I'm doing right there at that second and start cleaning. That's the only way I can take my frustration out.

Ms. B.:	Why do you have an IEP [individual education program]?
C:	I think it's because of my . . . I call it a learning disability. I really don't know what you would call it. I think it's because of my level of reading and the way I comprehend things.
K:	I have ADD.
Ms. B.:	What does that mean?
K:	Attention deficit disorder.
Ms. B.:	Do you take medication for that?
K:	No. I quit taking it because I was taking Ritalin and it didn't help at all, and they found I was better off of it.
L:	Well, the teachers, back when I was little, you know, they used to say I had ADD. My dad didn't want to believe it. And they gave me a test to check. And it turns out I didn't have ADD. I had short-term memory loss. So, you know, I have a hard time remembering things. But I think I worked things out in a way so it's not such a big problem anymore.
Ms. B.:	Do you write things down?
L:	No, I just . . . I don't know. It's still there, but it's not as big a problem anymore. It's something you work to overcome.
Ms. B.:	How do you feel about that—having an IEP?
C:	It doesn't bother me. It used to really bother me, because over at [middle school] I had two Englishes and then I was always in a study hall here, and it kind of bothered me to begin with, but then again it really didn't because I see that I needed the help. But I had to want to do it for myself. I couldn't let somebody else help me.
K:	I think it's fine. I mean, it's not a regular diploma. It's not a standard or advanced, but it's a diploma.
Ms. B.:	So you're going to get an IEP diploma?
K:	Yeah. But it's a diploma. And it's just like a regular one. It doesn't have the word IEP on it.
Ms. B.:	Do you think your IEP is helpful to you?
C:	I think it is if I'd use it. Sometimes I won't use it, as you found out. I've got to want to ask for help.
K:	Yes, I do.
L:	Yeah. It gives me resource to get stuff done. And oftentimes in, like, math—and math is my weak point—I'll need help, a lot of help. And that gives me help.
Ms. B.:	Some people say that we should do away with special education altogether and everyone should be in a regular class. How do you feel about that?

C: I think that's a little silly, because not everybody learns the same way as somebody else would, because I definitely don't catch on to what people are saying quickly. I think we should have the special education thing because, if everybody learned at the same level school would go by so much faster, but, you know, it doesn't. And everybody comprehends things at a different pace, and we all need somebody to teach us differently.

K: I think they're wrong when they say that, because. . . . Take me and [another student] who are in special education, and put them in regular classes with regular people. They're going to get made fun of if they don't know the answers. Because I'm going through that now in one of my regular classes.

L: I disagree. Because some kids are smarter, and some kids are not as smart. That's just the way things are. People like to believe that everyone's equal, but in reality they're not.

Ms. B.: Why do you think some kids abuse drugs and alcohol?

C: I think some say it has to do with their parents or peer pressure and things like that. I can honestly say, and I know you've probably heard this from a lot of kids, but I've never really done drugs. I have drank, I'll admit to that. I've been scared because my father used to do alcohol and used to do weed and stuff like that, and I've always been ascared that I'd get addicted to it, and I don't really want to ruin my life like that. I just don't understand why you would waste your life. . . . But some people, they'll start off with a little weed and then it goes to worse things, and then they really realize what they did, but it's peer pressure. [This school] definitely has a lot of that, because there are parties and the parties aren't directly chaperoned. There are a lot of parties that are illegal and have so much stuff, and freshmen go to them, and, they're like, "I'm gonna be cool," and the little freshmen want to fit in with the big seniors. So they try something . . . and then it leads to something worse.

K: Because they think it's something that's going to help them, and it's not.

Ms. B.: Why do you think that?

K: Because . . . it just makes your mind light-headed. The only reason that I know that is my brother was in a bad accident a couple years ago. He had been drinking and got behind the wheel of a car, and I vowed I'd never do it.

L: It's kind of like an escape, probably. Some kids do it because it makes them feel older. It makes them feel. . . . I don't know. I don't do drugs or alcohol. I've drunk before, but not often, and it's not that big a deal, and I don't do it at all anymore. I've never done drugs, and I never will. And that's because of my sister. The problem with things like drugs or weed or any of that stuff is that when you're a teenager, part of being a teenager is having these ups and downs on an emotional scale. When you're a teenager you cry a lot and laugh a lot at the same time. And what drugs do is dull that, and you go through your whole teenage life without that experience. So you don't develop like a normal person does. So you can be 34 or 40 and still be 17 mentally, because you never went through that whole stage in your life, because you dulled it. I just look at it as a complete waste of time, you know. They spend hundreds of dollars on this habit, and they just sit around with each other and smoke their weed or whatever . . . and the feelings are artificial. I believe in the good feelings that I already have. Some people get a buzz off the chemical the brain produces when you exercise a lot, they get addicted to it, and that's a good addiction. . . . Sometimes I've even gotten a buzz off music, just getting good feelings, I just felt so happy, and it's uplifting. Some people get a buzz off skiing. It just depends on what part of life your drug is. I don't believe in these other things.

Ms. B.: We just finished our state testing program. Some kids will pass and some won't. Do you think these tests are good for the school and for students?

C: I think people will see them as good for the school, because they can see if teachers are doing their job. Which I don't believe. I don't think any kid really likes the SOLs [standards of learning tests]. Technically, if they do, well . . . they like tests. I don't like them because I don't think they're fair to students, because students like me, I know I freak out when you have a big test coming up. . . . I don't deal too well with pressure. It's not fair, because you don't really know how the teacher's teaching, because you don't know if the teacher taught you all you should know. . . . If you don't pass the SOLs, then you can't graduate, and I don't think that's too fair. It's too much pressure on us.

L: I don't really care. SOLs are a joke to me. They're so easy. If you don't pass them, then you really don't deserve to pass the school, because they're so pathetically easy. They don't even mention them in advanced and honors classes. They know the kids are more than prepared to crush the tests.

Ms. B.: Do you have siblings?

L: I have an older sister. She's four years older than me. She's 23.

Ms. B.: Do you think school was harder for you than it was for your sister?

L:	At first, she was better at school. She used to get straight As. And I used to be the one that did poorly in school. And then, ever since she hit a certain age she started mixing in with the wrong people and her grades dropped, you know, she started getting into really bad stuff, and then she had a baby and then she dropped out of school. So it was, like, for a while she was the better one, and it switched all of a sudden, and then she became the rotten apple.
Ms. B.:	So, do you think you learned something from that? From seeing her get mixed up with the wrong people?
L:	Oh, yes, absolutely. Because she did that, I am very firm in the belief that I'll never do any of the stuff she did, like drugs. She's completely irresponsible, and she made the worst possible choices and got with the worst people you can imagine. Like, my nephew's father is in prison right now. And I just don't ever want to become her.
Ms. B.:	How about your parents and grandparents—do you know anything about how school was for them?
L:	My Brazilian grandparents, I don't know them very well at all. I hardly ever see them. And I only met my grandma once, and she wasn't really my grandma. She's my step-grandmother, I suppose. My Brazilian grandpa died. . . . I probably met him, but I was too young to remember. . . . I don't know what the deal was with her. They probably didn't go to school much at all. My American grandparents, I know my grandmother, she only has a middle school education. So, from there, she dropped out and married my grandpa. And I'm not really sure about his education. He joined the military.

Questions About the Case

1. What do you think about Carrie's response to Ms. Brigham's first question? How would you talk to Carrie about changing her attitude?
2. What do you think of Carrie's and Larry's comments about the SOL ("standards of learning") tests? (The name of the state-wide tests vary from state to state.) How do you view such tests as a teacher, and what do you think teachers should say to students about them?
3. How would you respond to Kate's comments about being in a special class?

12

Cases on Anxiety and Related Disorders

Kane's personal description gives us a small window into the experience of one person with Tourette's syndrome (TS) (also known as Tourette's disorder) and the way it is related to internal states. The experience of TS, like the experience of any other disorder, is highly individual. The attentional and obsessive-compulsive aspects of TS, however, appear to be common themes in people's first-person accounts.

Kane

My Tourette's syndrome began 19 years ago, when I was 7. It started with head jerking, but then I started having other symptoms too, including facial tics, tics involving my arms and legs, vocal tics like squeaking and grunting, and tics that involved touching things. I took haloperidol (marketed under the name Haldol, an antipsychotic drug sometimes given to control tics) from the time I was 11 until I was 13, but eventually I was prescribed clonidine (trade name Catapres, often prescribed for high blood pressure) because of the side effects of the Haldol. One year later, clonidine was deemed ineffective and all medication was discontinued.

Maybe I can best describe the sensation of having TS as hyperattention to my body: not so much like an itch as a constant bombardment of bodily sensations. In my experience, having TS is like being in a state of keen bodily awareness, or a continual consciousness of sensations in your muscles, joints, and skin. When all of my tics are suppressed, almost all of my joints and muscles begin to demand my attention. Having TS builds up to a stiffening feeling, so that my skin feels like a hardened casing and my joints feel like they're becoming rigid. The intensity of these feelings increases until they become so unpleasant and distracting that I'm relieved by my tics. This compulsion to do the tics is like feeling that you have to scratch a severe itch.

The reason that tics bring only partial relief, however, is that unlike scratching an itch the tics don't relieve the hyperattention for long. Tics just make the TS go back to baseline for a while. So doing the tics isn't really pleasant either, but doing them does give you temporary relief from the persistent hyperawareness.

Source: Rewritten from Kane (1994)

Questions About the Case

1. If you had a student in your class who began showing stereotyped movements, what should be your response (i.e., what should you do, how should you handle it)?
2. How would you describe the relationship between TS and attention problems?
3. How could you best show understanding and support for a student with TS?

◆ ◆ ◆

Sometimes, students with anxiety disorders perform rituals or routines that may seem almost tic-like in their compulsion and repetition. Usually, the rituals associated with the anxious state are thought by the individual who performs them to ward off evil, prevent undesirable events, or create conditions for something good to happen. Anxiety disorders sometimes occur along with other disorders. Sometimes, the anxiety is very responsive to medication, but occasionally medication does not result in significant improvement. Teachers who deal with severely anxious students may need to create a classroom environment in which the student feels safe and in which the rituals associated with anxiety have a minimum effect on academic progress.

Seth

Seth had a long list of "habits," even as a 14-year-old. His habits were rituals he felt compelled to do to keep something bad from happening. For example, in coming to school he had to cross multiple thresholds to get to his classroom. Going through doorways was extremely difficult for Seth, and he did little dances at each threshold before going through the doorway. Tiled hallways were a nightmare for Seth because each crack potentially represented a line he shouldn't cross. He dealt with tiled floors by concentrating on only certain seams, and it was impossible for anyone observing his behavior to figure out in advance which seam would cause him to stop and do a little ritual dance before crossing it.

The bad things that might happen if he didn't do his rituals before crossing a threshold or crack in the flooring or before submitting an answer on an academic assignment (he did a lot of ritual erasing and ritual movements of his pencil in completing academic work) centered mainly on his family. He was fearful that if he omitted any ritual (or "habit"), someone in his family, especially his mother, would have a terrible accident.

Antianxiety medication helped Seth somewhat, but he still had a very difficult time in school. Although he was a highly intelligent boy, his academic work was not up to expectations. This was primarily because he could not open a book, turn to a specific page, or do written assignments without going through elaborate rituals (e.g., opening and closing the book, turning and returning the page, making motions with his pencil above the paper, erasing and rewriting answers). While his classmates were proceeding with their work as usual, Seth was routinely far behind schedule in getting his work done.

Questions About the Case

1. If you were Seth's teacher, how would you respond to his ritualistic behavior?
2. What do you see as the most important differences between Seth's behavior and TS?
3. How would you deal with classmates who tease Seth about his odd behavior?

◆ ◆ ◆

We ordinarily think about special schools as having particular value for students with acting-out behavior. Special classes and special schools, however, also provide environments where students with internalizing disorders feel safe and can flower.

Pauline

Pauline came to school her first day in a special school for students with emotional or behavioral disorders (EBDs) looking bedraggled. At age 14, she was tall and slender. But she hobbled in looking more like a wounded crow than like a graceful swan.

She'd experienced nothing but trauma during her past three years in high school. Because she was tall for her age, she had very quickly become the butt of jokes among her peers. The jokes turned to bullying, including not just verbal taunts but physical attacks. Teachers tried to intervene, but the packs of students hunting for her always found their target, and she seemed always to become the victim of her abusive peers.

Pauline had been a socially outgoing, average student who was always eager to contribute in class. But because of the teasing and bullying from her peers, she became withdrawn and pale, with her shoulders hunched and too frightened to speak or to be spoken to for fear of ridicule. When her teachers—who were unaware of the hard time her peers were giving her—urged her to become more active in class, she became distraught. School no longer seemed like a safe place to her, and she was often truant. When her parents discovered what was happening, they forced her to go to school every day. They took her to school themselves. Pauline was under such stress that she started to vomit when she had to go to school. This made her peer group turn on her even more, even to start blocking the bathroom when Pauline needed to throw up. If a teacher passed by when they were keeping Pauline out of the bathroom, her peers pretended to be helping her so the teacher wouldn't interfere.

Pauline's emotional trauma didn't cause her to become aggressive, but it certainly reflected a disturbed child who found her whole school environment disturbing and alien. She was in such a mental state that she began underachieving in all her classes. Some of the teachers suggested that she had specific learning difficulties. She was failing to thrive in school, and she existed merely as a lonely, hyperanxious, vulnerable child. She had lost her dignity.

The educational psychologist suggested an alternative placement in a special school for students with EBD. After a few weeks in the special school, Pauline began to interact more with the teachers. She never spoke up in class, but after a lesson ended she'd hang around to discuss some point with the teacher. The teachers soon saw that she didn't have any significant learning disabilities.

Pauline's attendance was good. Gradually, her pallor began to fade and her eyes lost some of their traumatized glare. Eventually, she told the school counselor about her personal pain and anguish over the previous three years in the regular high school. She described her experiences as being like "a daily nightmare." She was totally disoriented in the high school of 1,500 students. She described herself as having been "floating in a sea of people" once her peers turned on her.

In the small special school of 40 students, Pauline found peace. She learned to trust people again—first adults, and then her fellow students. She became an active participant the classroom, no longer just the peripheral onlooker. Her capacity to care for others became clear, and she befriended many isolated individuals.

She spent just two years in the special school. She left at the age of 16, and not all of her problems had been solved. After all, in two years it's impossible to make up for three lost years. New situations or changes in routines still caused Pauline anxiety. But when she left the school, she had a renewed sense of self-worth. This "restrictive environment" had been her safe haven. It had allowed her to recover her dignity.

Source: Rewritten from Carpenter and Bovair (1996)

Questions About the Case

1. How would you respond to someone's argument that Pauline belonged in a general education class in a general education school, not the special school?
2. If you were a teacher in a general education school, how would you respond to bullying of students like Pauline?
3. What would be required to make all schools small, supportive, and inviting places for students like Pauline?

Students with anxiety disorders seem especially puzzling to many people. Their problems strike us as unnecessary because social interactions or being part of a large group seems so natural and effortless to most of us. But, as in the case of stuttering and some other language fluency problems, "relaxing" and other admonitions from others are often unhelpful. In the following case, Mr. Vazquez, who contributed the personal reflections feature for the textbook chapter on anxiety and related disorders, interviews one of his students.

Mr. Vazquez Interviews John

Mr. Vazquez: John, tell me about your feelings about your high school.

John: I don't really like the school because it is so large but I do like my friends and teachers . . . most of them. I also do enjoy being able to eat lunch in the classroom instead of the cafeteria. Too many people that I don't know.

Mr. V:	What are some of the things that you would like to change about the school?
J:	I would like to be able to only have one class for everything. I mean I would like to stay in one area and not have to worry about if something is going to happen.
Mr. V:	Have you always felt like "something" was going to happen to you that was bad before you came to the high school?
J:	I really don't think that wanting to know what is going to happen is a problem. I don't feel that I ever had a problem before I came to the high school. No one told me about this problem.
Mr. V:	So you don't feel like you have a problem?
J:	I think sometimes I am just overreacting. My parents and you teachers feel like I have a problem.

Questions About the Case

1. In what ways are John's responses to this interview typical of students with anxiety disorders?
2. What would you say about John's being required to attend a regular class?
3. Why do you think John doesn't see himself as having a problem but his parents and teachers feel he does? Which perspective on his behavior (John's versus that of his parents and teachers) do you think should be the basis for John's individual education program (IEP)?

CASE

13

Cases on Depression and Suicidal Behavior

Often, it's difficult to understand depression because it seems unreasonable to us. Children, youth, or even adults who are depressed may seem to others to have a completely irrational view of the world and to be frightened of things that are extremely unlikely to happen. We think that if they'd only come to their senses, they wouldn't be depressed. Occasionally, we can see reasons—or, at least think we see reasons—for the depression.

Buddy

As a 10-year-old, Buddy shows a lot of the signs of depression. He talks a lot about how sad he is, he's socially withdrawn, he doesn't like to watch or play sports, and he often complains of aches and pains that his parents and doctor can't explain (as growing pains or illness or injury). Lately, he's become increasingly disinterested in school. His scores on standardized tests are as high as ever, but now he's getting failing grades in classes in which he once did well. Actually, his father and mother separated not long ago, and since they did, his grades have plummeted. His parents separated after years of bitter conflict, which eventually devolved into arguing, accusations, and even hitting. Before they separated, Buddy's parents admitted that they were preoccupied with their own relationship and had little interaction with Buddy. Both of Buddy's parents have had bouts of depression, and his mother is in psychotherapy and is taking antidepressants. Buddy seems to think he's responsible for his parents' conflict and separation and worries that they'll never get back together. Buddy's father visits him every week, but Buddy's afraid that every visit is the last and that he'll never see his father again. He misses his mother when he is in school and constantly worries about her being okay.

Rewritten from Stark, Ostrander, Kurowski, Swearer, and Bowen (1995)

Questions About the Case

1. In what ways is Buddy's case typical of children experiencing depression?
2. What do you think were the primary causal factors contributing to Buddy's depression?

3. Supposing that you were Buddy's teacher, how would you respond (what would you do) to deal most effectively with his anxiety and depression?

Sometimes, depression or suicide seems so uncharacteristic of someone that it surprises us. It's like a person goes through a transformation, and now falls into a depression over stressful situations that previously he or she would have been able to handle. Something seems to send this individual over the edge.

Stanlea

Stanlea was the only child of a military couple. His mother and father, both retired army captains, knew routine and discipline. They provided a stable, kind, and loving but strict, no-nonsense environment for Stanlea from the time he was an infant. He grew up happy and successful academically and athletically. When he was a young boy, his mother was diagnosed with muscular dystrophy. By the time he was in middle school, she had become severely physically disabled.

By the time he was a high school junior, Stanlea was liked by teachers and admired by his peers. He got As and Bs in virtually every subject, never any grade less than a C, and he played multiple sports very well. He went to church regularly and was a Boy Scout. He was very helpful and reliable in caring for his mother. He seemed destined for graduation in the top tier of his class and admission to a good college. He was loving and respectful toward his parents, seldom causing them even minor concern. He was never in any serious trouble at home or at school.

But, then—in the middle of his junior year—he made a misstep. He had never bought or used drugs, but he bought, from another student, a legal substance that was said to mimic the effects of marijuana. Although this substance was not illegal, it was prohibited by the local school board, something Stanlea knew. Another student reported his purchase, and the substance was found in Stanlea's possession. Stanlea was then suspended under the school's zero-tolerance policy. A hearing for his case was scheduled by the school board.

At the hearing, weeks after he had been suspended from school, Stanlea was apologetic and remorseful. He admitted his guilt and promised never again to do what he now called such a "stupid" thing. He felt that he had let down his parents and the school. His parents felt that he had committed an infraction of school rules and that he should be disciplined, but they felt his previous good behavior and accomplishments should be taken into consideration and that he should be allowed to return to his school.

The school board was unsympathetic. Claiming strict adherence to their disciplinary procedures, they refused to budge, regardless of any extenuating circumstances or prior behavior. In spite of his parents' support and pleas, the school board stuck to its guns. Stanlea was expelled from the school he had been attending. He was allowed to continue his education in the district, but he was required to go to a different high school. That is, he was allowed to return to school after his suspension, but only to a school in which he had not committed an infraction and hence where he had no "record" or history of misconduct for which there was zero tolerance.

Stanlea became bitter and morose after the school board's decision. Cut off from his former friends, teachers, and activities, he became increasingly depressed and socially withdrawn. After a few days at his new school, he killed himself. Many people, including Stanlea's parents, thought the matter had been handled very poorly by the schools. The school board and superintendent maintained that their zero-tolerance policy and disciplinary process had nothing to do with Stanlea's suicide.

Based on St. George (2011)

Questions About the Case

1. What role do you think the district's zero-tolerance policy and disciplinary decision had in Stanlea's suicide?
2. If you had been responsible for Stanlea's discipline, what would have been your decision? Why?
3. What do you think Stanlea's father or mother could have done to deal with Stanlea's depression and withdrawal following the school board's decision?

Without anticipating problems, teachers may find themselves working with depressed or suicidal students. Too often, problems are ignored until they become undeniable and very dramatic.

Jackie

Jackie is a little fourth grader, but she's a terror. She somehow manages to do acceptable academic work, so she's never been diagnosed as having an emotional or behavioral disorder (EBD). But she's refused teachers' instructions since she started school, and the way she behaves she could be considered to exhibit oppositional defiant disorder (ODD). She may be little, but she's strong, and other kids are afraid of her. She pushes and hits and threatens them, so they keep their distance. She has no real friends. Sometimes, she bangs her head on her desk or the floor and shouts things like, "I'm no good!" or "I want to die!" This really "freaks out" the other students. Jackie has been evaluated for special education, but she was evaluated only after she had been terrorizing her classmates and teachers for years. Her latest stunt was tying the cord of a classroom window blind around her neck and jumping off a table, bringing the blind crashing down. When she did this, there was a substitute teacher in the room. The sub considered this suicidal.

Rewritten from Kauffman, Lloyd, Baker, and Riedel (1995)

Questions About the Case

1. What do you see as the essence of Jackie's problems?
2. What would have been required (at various ages or earlier grades) to prevent Jackie's fourth-grade behavior problems?
3. Given Jackie's behavior now, what suggestions do you have for her teacher?

◆ ◆ ◆

Depressed and suicidal students are often difficult for teachers to draw out. They may be especially reluctant to reveal their feelings, and it may take careful probing to find out what students think or feel about things. Here, Tezella Cline, the teacher who wrote the personal reflections for the chapter on depression and suicidal behavior for the textbook, interviews a student named George.

Tezella Cline Interviews George

Ms. Cline:	How are you feeling today?
George:	Good.
Ms. C:	How would you describe yourself?
G:	Trapped up in feelings.
Ms. C:	Can you tell me about any of those?
G:	Like, different ones. Like, wanting to go home, but my mom hadn't came yet.
Ms. C:	Name and describe things that make you feel the best about yourself.
G:	I like working alone. And . . . when I'm doing a good job and the teacher says that I'm doing a good job.
Ms. C:	Describe your personality.
G:	I think I'm a nice guy. When you get to know me a good bit. And generous.
Ms. C:	Tell me about your life.
G:	There have been ups and downs all through it. I had to go to Alexander.
Ms. C:	What's Alexander?
G:	Children's Center . . . and then I had to go back home to live with my mom. I was in regular classes, then I went to BEH [behaviorally and emotionally handicapped classes], and that's all. There have been ups and downs in my life.
Ms. C:	How do you feel about those ups and downs?

G: Well, when I went to Alexander, I didn't like it. It was a children's center where they kept me overnight for 60 days.

Ms. C: When did you go there?

G: I think when I was like 4 or 5. I was out of control.

Ms. C: Out of control? What do you mean by that?

G: I was, like, being too bad to stay at home.

Ms. C: And at school? What was it like there?

G: I was in a regular class, and I didn't do very good in school. I got suspended a lot.

Ms. C: How often do you think you got suspended?

G: I got in trouble with the teacher, like, more than once every day.

Ms. C: Can you describe for me some of the types of things that you did?

G: I would not follow directions and not respect the teachers. I would mostly talk to my peers. Not listen to the teacher.

Ms. C: But all kids do that sometimes, right?

G: Yeah.

Ms. C: But what made you different?

G: I was doing it constantly.

Ms. C: Tell me the best thing about your life right now.

G: That I have a loving family that cares about me.

Ms. C: Do you have friends?

G: Yeah! I do!

Ms. C: Tell me about your friends.

G: They're fun, and I talk to them.

Ms. C: You don't have to name them, but describe your friends.

G: Some of them are bad, and some of them are good.

Ms. C: Which ones do you like to be with the most? Be honest.

G: Sometimes the bad.

Ms. C: What makes you say that they are bad?

G: Their actions are bad.

Ms. C: For example . . .

G: Like they do bad things when they know it's wrong. Then they try to cover up for it.

Ms. C: What kinds of things?

G: Like, they throw spitballs or something like that.

Ms. C: What do you like best about being in school?

G: The math.

Ms. C: Why?

G: Because that's my favorite subject.

Ms. C: How do you feel when you're doing your favorite subject?

G: It makes me feel good 'cause I know what I'm doing most of the time.

Ms. C: What kinds of expressions do you have when you're doing math?

G: Like algebra and stuff like that?

Ms. C: No, I mean what kinds of emotions?

G: I'm feeling good because I know that I know how to do this and it's fun.

Ms. C: What do you like best about being at home?

G: All the privileges that I get, and I know I can't do that in a group home or something like that.

Ms. C: So you do think about that sometimes?

G: Yes, when my mom reminds me about it a lot.

Ms. C: How do you feel when you have to do subjects that you do not want to do?

G: I feel mad sometimes at the teacher, but I try to do it the best I can.

Ms. C: When you do those subjects that you don't like, tell me what you might be thinking.

G: I'm thinking that I don't want to do it, but I've got to 'cause I want to learn.

Ms. C: How do you handle those feelings when you feel them coming?

G: I try to ignore them because I need to do my work.

Ms. C: Do you talk to yourself?

G: Yes.

Ms. C: What do you say?

G: "I can do it." I give myself strategies saying that I can do it and stuff like that.

Ms. C: What kind of strategies have you learned through the years?

G: That if you talk to yourself enough that you will convince yourself that you can do it.

Ms. C: Tell me the things that you say, specifically.

G: "I can do it, and you're the one that can do it."

Ms. C: Now, think about when you are angry and you're not saying those things to yourself. What kinds of things are you saying?

G: When I'm angry, I'm mostly angry at somebody and it gets me really mad. And I'm not thinking about nothing, and I just say things that I don't really mean.

Ms. C: Right. What kinds of things come out?

G: Sometimes I curse.

Ms. C: After you've said things that you don't really mean, then what are you feeling? Do you feel good, or do you feel bad?

G: I feel bad because I've blown up at my mom a lot, and then at the end I'm really sad that I did that, and I can't live with myself sometimes doing that. So I need to stop doing it.

Ms. C: You have a lot of emotions going on there. Think now specifically about how you feel when you're getting angry or upset. What's usually the first feeling on up to where it's the top feeling?

G: That I'm really getting mad at somebody . . . like I'm saying I can cool down a little bit. Whenever I get to the top of it, I get really, really mad, and then I get like saying, "*Rurrr,*" and I get, like, shaking all over and my face starts to turn red and stuff like that.

Ms. C: When you reach that point, what are you thinking?

G: That I should, like, sometimes I think that I need to hit the person, but I know in myself that I shouldn't because I'll get suspended from school.

Ms. C: So what do you do?

G: I tell myself that you shouldn't hit 'cause it's not the right thing to do.

Ms. C: Have you ever told yourself the right thing but then done the other?

G: Yeah. I do that a lot. Then I think I know the right thing, then whenever I be bad I think it's a little more funner, sometimes.

Ms. C: So it makes you feel . . .

G: Happy sometimes when I be bad, but whenever I get the consequences, it don't make sense to me.

Ms. C: Okay. Think about when you're angry. You told me what you're telling yourself. What ways do you show others that you're angry?

G: I really have a high temper. I mean, I yell a lot. Sometimes I throw things.

Ms. C: So explain this to me. Are you saying that it's not always when you have to do work, or you have to do things that other people tell you to do that get you angry?

G: No, it's not like that. It's like almost every day I try to deal with it to a certain extent.

Ms. C: So sometimes, even when you're doing something that you like to do, you get mad?

G: Yeah, I get angry then, too.

Ms. C: Do you ever get mad at yourself?

G: Yeah. I get mad at myself 'cause I can't do it myself, sometimes. That makes me mad at myself.

Ms. C: When you get mad at yourself, how does that make you feel toward yourself? Do you ever do things to yourself or say negative things to yourself?

G: Yeah, like right after I get done yelling at my mom when we have a big fight, I say, I tell it to myself, I say, "Why did you do that? You shouldn't have done that 'cause she's your mom. And you shouldn't say those kind of things to your mom." And I get real mad at myself sometimes.

Ms. C: Do you ever feel like hurting yourself or something like that?

G: At one point in my life I did. I thought I couldn't live with myself doing this. And I thought that I should kill myself, but I didn't.

Ms. C: Do you remember how old you were when you thought that?

G: I think I was around 6 or 5.

Ms. C: That young?

G: Yeah.

Ms. C: Since then, have you ever tried to hurt yourself in any way?

G: Well, there was this one time I was sitting in a car and I had a knife. I cut my finger. Right across here.

Ms. C: Have you ever felt just really, really low or really sad?

G: Yes.

Ms. C: Have you ever felt, would you say, depressed?

G: Yes. I felt that way a lot when I was really young.

Ms. C: Can you use any words to describe how that feels?

G: It feels like you can't go any lower than you go. You're, like, real low and you're saying to yourself, "Why can't I go on? What have I done?" And I just got so low, and it's hard to like, do stuff 'cause you're so depressed and you don't know what to do next.

Ms. C: What do teachers do that makes you feel this way sometimes?

G: When they tell you to do something over and over. They keep doing that over and over, and that gets me mad.

Ms. C: What do teachers do sometimes that makes you feel depressed or sad or low?

G: Whenever a teacher makes fun of me, it makes me feel sad or low.

Ms. C: What could teachers do to help make you feel better or feel lifted or happy once you're feeling depressed or sad or low?

G: Like, do my favorite subject, like math or something like that.

Ms. C: Name some things that you do at school that seem to get you into trouble.

G: I tend to hang with some bad people, bad friends. I shouldn't do that. I should know better.

Ms. C: Anything else that you do at school that gets you into trouble? What about in the classroom?

G: Yeah. I talk back, and I don't follow the teacher's directions.

Ms. C: What happens when you talk back or don't follow the teacher's directions? What comes after that?

G: I usually lose points or I get, like, a time-out.

Ms. C: How do you feel when that happens?

G: I feel angry at myself along with them [bad friends] because I didn't follow directions. And with them because they made me have to do it.

Ms. C: So even though you understand the rules and you know what is expected, then when you don't do what is expected and you get the consequence you still feel angry when you get the consequence?

G: Yes.

Ms. C: Now, is that anger directed to the teacher, do you think, or is it to yourself?

G: Mostly toward myself and also a little bit toward the teacher.

Ms. C: How do you react when you get caught doing something wrong?

G: Most of the time I say, "I didn't do it" or "It wasn't me."

Ms. C: Do you accept responsibility for your own behavior?

G: Sometimes. But I do not accept it more than I do accept it.

Ms. C: Do you tell the truth?

G: Sometimes.

Ms. C: Do you tell the truth about serious things?

G: Yes.

Ms. C: What kinds of things do you think you do not tell the truth about?

G: My behavior or something I did wrong.

Ms. C: Do you do your homework?

G: Sometimes, when I feel like it.

Ms. C: What makes you feel like doing it?

G: I want to get it over with so I can have time to play.

Ms. C: How do you feel about your school?

G: I feel like the school has lived up to its potential because it's been here so long and I think it's done good in all subjects. It teaches kids how to do good.

Ms. C: How do you feel about your class right now? The situation in your [self-contained] class right now?

G: I think we're not doing too good toward making the school's name that it's already got. Because we have a lot of problems in class. Behavior problems.

Ms. C: Describe the problems. What kinds of problems?

G: Behavior problems and temper moods. Tempers fly up, and we get mad at each other and mad at the teachers and stuff like that.

Ms. C: What do you think the teacher should do when the moods and tempers fly up?

G: The teacher should give them consequences and redirect them.

Ms. C: What are the things about your class that help you the most?

G: That some people in my class help me do my work. Group work.

Ms. C: What are some things in your class that upset you or make you angry?

G: When their tempers fly up at me and they think I did something and I didn't.

Ms. C: Do you have a routine in your class?

G: Yes. It's on our point system where we have to do math or social studies.

Ms. C: Do you think that's good for you?

G: Yeah. I like to know what is after each other so I can prepare for it. I think that's a good routine.

Ms. C: When you're feeling sad or depressed, how long does that feeling usually last?

G: Feeling angry and depressed, well, I'm never like that for a long period of time. For some reason my feelings never stay the same.

They never keep going on and on and on like some people. They last 5 minutes or less.

Ms. C: Do you always know what makes you sad or depressed? Or does it just sometimes come upon you?

G: It sometimes just comes on me at different times of the day.

Ms. C: When do you think you're the most up or happy?

G: In the morning.

Ms. C: Then when does that feeling of lowness or depression come on you?

G: In the afternoon. Especially after lunch 'cause that's when I have to take my medicine.

Ms. C: How does that make you feel?

G: It makes me feel not good 'cause I know I can't control my behavior without it. Makes me feel kind of depressed because I can't do it without it. It makes me feel not good at all.

Ms. C: How can teachers or other adults help you when you feel like hurting yourself or becoming aggressive?

G: Probably restrain the person.

Ms. C: How does that make you feel?

G: Angry.

Ms. C: How do you think it makes the teachers feel when they have to restrain you?

G: They are probably thinking the same thing.

Ms. C: What would you say to a person who was feeling hopeless and trying to hurt themselves?

G: You shouldn't do that because you have a life to live and God put you on this earth so you could live this life.

Ms. C: Think about a time when you were having a great day and then suddenly everything changed within you and you began feeling angry or sad. Can you explain why or how that happened?

G: Yeah. Like, when I was all happy and then I thought about my rabbit died 'cause my dog killed it. I started to feel sad, and then I got all angry at everybody and I took my anger out on them.

Ms. C: So, sounds like what causes you to have sad or depressed feelings is sometimes on the outside, but sometimes they are on the inside, too. And they have the same effect on you just like it's happening now. So it sounds like it's important to talk about your feelings before . . . to let people know what's going on.

G: Yeah, I think it is because you can let people know before you explode. So they'll know what to expect.

Ms. C: Is talking to your teacher important?

G: Yes, I think it is because you can let your feelings out and you can express to them how you feel.

Ms. C: Name three things that you love about school.

G: Math, science, and technology.

Ms. C: Name three things that you really dislike about school.

G: Social studies and reading.

Ms. C: How do rules make you feel?

G: Feels like we are trapped. You can do this, but you can't do that. It makes you feel like you're restricted to certain things.

Ms. C: And then, as a result of that feeling, what other feelings come? What do you feel like doing if you feel trapped?

G: It feels like you can't get out of here, you can't move, and stuff like that.

Questions About the Case

1. What diagnoses might George have received besides depression?
2. If a student is misbehaving in school, what would lead you to suspect depression rather than another disorder as the primary problem?
3. In what ways do you think a special class might help a student who is experiencing depression, and in what ways might a special class contribute to the student's depression rather than help?

CASE

14

Cases on Severe Mental Disorders

Wanda was diagnosed with childhood schizophrenia and reported having auditory hallucinations—hearing buildings and other objects talk to her. Excessive fantasies can make a student very difficult to teach, if not inaccessible to teaching. Note the frustration of Wanda's teacher.

Wanda

I wasn't ready for 11-year-old Wanda, even though I knew that emotionally disturbed children sometimes have wild fantasies. Wanda had an IQ in the gifted range, but her high intelligence didn't seem to do her much good. Maybe it expanded her fantasies, but it didn't seem to apply much to reality. I never found a topic of conversation, a part of the school curriculum, a place, or a time that wasn't part of her bizarre imagination. She fantasized about jeans. For example, she said she had special 40-pocket and 100-pocket jeans with zippers in the front. She drew pictures of them. She had fantasies about the president and the governor and crucifixes and the story *The Pit and the Pendulum*. She fantasized about doctors, nurses, swimming pools, toilets, injections, physical exams, and more. She had fantasies about her moles (one on her arm was a microphone that she used for broadcasting, and one on her leg was a thermostat that she said controlled her body temperature).

When Wanda was fantasizing, she got a peculiar, fixed grin on her face, her eyes looked glazed, she giggled, and she talked in a high-pitched squeaky voice to imaginary friends. She often drew pictures with captions representing fantasy objects and activities. Sometimes she engaged in other bizarre behaviors, such as flattening herself on the floor or wall, kissing it, caressing it, and talking to it. I couldn't teach Wanda or have a rational conversation with her while she was fantasizing, and she was "in" fantasy almost all the time, so my problem as a teacher was serious. When she wasn't "in" fantasy, I found it impossible to predict when she'd suddenly enter her fantasy world again.

Rewritten from Patton, Blackbourn, Kauffman, and Brown (1991)

89

Questions About the Case

1. How was Wanda typical and how was she not typical of children diagnosed with schizophrenia?
2. If you were Wanda's teacher, how would you respond to her fantasies?
3. If you were going to intervene to prevent or control Wanda's fantasies, how would you try to do so?

◆ ◆ ◆

Teachers can often reach children who have schizophrenia in surprising ways. Here a teacher describes some of the eccentricities of a girl who is clearly highly talented in many ways, some of which are related to her disability. The teacher sees past the odd behavior of this student and values her as an interesting, endearing human being. The student's response to the teacher's acceptance of her as a person is not surprising in many ways, although it was long in coming. Working with students who have severe mental disorders is not likely to be rewarding for teachers who expect quick breakthroughs.

Carmen

Carmen is a very unusual third grader, clearly unique. She is extraordinarily bright, years ahead of her grade level in every academic area. She devours books of every genre. She reads Proust and Kafka, Seuss and Shakespeare. She knows the periodic table cold. She has a mastery of world history that would put most adults to shame. She is a dream student.

Carmen is also schizophrenic. Hers eyes shine with an unnatural, often unnerving brightness. Her appearance varies wildly from one day to the next. Pajama bottoms with a sweater, flip-flops, and thousands of braids one day, a white communion dress with snow boots and a winter hat the next. Her gait and posture are off in a way that nobody can pinpoint exactly.

Another important thing you need to know about Carmen is that she has many personas. At school, we are most likely to see the Baptist minister, the opera singer, the mime, and the 19th-century British naturalist. Really. Other Carmen variants include an elderly man with dementia, an FBI agent, and an African elephant. These don't come to school often, for some reason.

I'm filled with anticipation each morning as I wait to discover which Carmen will get off the short bus. If Baptist-preacher-Carmen descends the steep bus steps, that is who I will be teaching all day. Preacher days play out something like this:

Me:	Good morning, Carmen!
Carmen (Baptist-preacher girl):	Yes, indeed, it is a grand morning, Miz H. Praise the Lord! Hallelujah! Amen! Put your hands in the air and testify!

Me:	How are you this morning, Carmen?
Carmen:	I am steeped in sin like all mankind, Miz H. But by the graces of our Lord I am here to live another day!
Me:	Well, that is fine news indeed. Let's head to the classroom and start our day!
Carmen, testifying:	Lord, yes, let's. An education is a righteous and Godly gift, ma'am.

All 56 pounds of this kid somehow manage to produce the exact voice of an evangelical Baptist preacher at a well-attended tent revival. It's eerie, but fascinating. Her voice deepens until she sounds like a large man. Her cadence, tone, and delivery are dead-on. If she had her own TV ministry, she would be raking in big money.

I adore Carmen, utterly and completely. She knows this, and it is the only reason I am able to teach her anything at all. Lessons with Carmen present bizarre challenges. It takes a whole lot of extra time to work on adding fractions with unlike denominators when we must praise the lord and yell hallelujah every few minutes. It is also much more fun this way. Teaching Carmen always stretches my skills to the limit and often exceeds them. Still, Carmen teaches me so much more than I will ever impart to her.

Recently I was giving Carmen the annual assessments required of all special education students. British-naturalist-Carmen was eager to tackle the questions and more than willing to give it her all. About an hour into our evaluation session, I read one of the assessment items incorrectly. Quickly I apologized, said that I would reread the question, and assured Carmen that the situation was my fault entirely. At these words, Carmen inexplicably jumped up, knocking over her chair in the process, and became very agitated. She began pacing the small room and wringing her hands, behaviors I recognized as signs of extreme stress.

"No, no, no, not at all your fault. Quite not your fault!" she proclaimed in a perfect, upper-class British accent.

"Okay," I agreed calmly—knowing better than to contradict Carmen in this condition—"It is not my fault at all."

"Right!" she exclaimed emphatically, pounding her fist on the table for good measure. "It is obviously the fault of the republic."

I was baffled and amazed by her declaration. I sat quietly, looked interested, and waited. Experience had taught me that this was the best course of action when Carmen was worked up. (Or, as British-naturalist-Carmen would say, whenever she had her knickers in a knot.)

Carmen went on, accent sounding like the narrator on a documentary detailing the insect life of Great Britain, "As you see, some person of very great elevation told a slightly less significant person who told a more minor person who told another smaller person who told somebody even closer to the bottom of the totem pole that students like myself must take this test. The lowest person instructed you to give me the test. It all started with the leader of the republic, and there is where the fault must be placed."

"I never thought of it that way," I admitted honestly. "You have amazing ideas and such a phenomenal way of seeing the world."

Carmen did something utterly unexpected then. She hugged me for the first and only time in our years together. She stood, tears pooling in her eyes, and said simply, "Thank you. Thank you for listening to me. For hearing me. For knowing that just because I'm crazy, it doesn't mean I'm wrong." This time she spoke in her own voice. I'd never heard her speak without one of her personas to shield her before. Her voice was beautiful, lilting, strong, and her very own.

Contributed by Betty Hallenbeck

Questions About the Case

1. How do you think Carmen would respond to a regular classroom and a regular classroom teacher? Why?
2. If you were Carmen's teacher, how would you respond to her various personas?
3. What do you think of the teacher's response to Carmen's agitation at the teacher's error? Why? What alternatives would you suggest, and what do you think would have been the outcome?

Sometimes children eventually diagnosed with schizophrenia are first diagnosed with other problems. And sometimes medication and special education are very helpful in coping with schizophrenia.

Bill

Bill was a colicky baby whose problems were already apparent. He seemed to be in constant motion, and he engaged frequently in repetitive head-banging. As a toddler and young child he needed constant supervision because of his high level of inappropriate behavior. He was unpredictable and destructive. For example, he hurt the family pets and set fires. When he was just 6 years old, he was placed in a special school for children with learning disabilities. Besides his other problems, his visual-motor behavior was developmentally delayed.

Later, Bill's behavior became increasingly bizarre and problematic. He started defecating and urinating in odd places. He started scratching and hitting himself. He cried and threw himself against walls. He became preoccupied with germs, death, and sex, and panicked if he was separated from his mother. When he was about 8, Bill's language became illogical and difficult to follow. His talk tended to drift to morbid themes. He seemed to be hallucinating at home and at school. One time he claimed to see blood oozing from the walls and floors, and because of this hallucination he frantically tried to tear the walls and floor apart. He started playing with knives. He talked about killing himself, and one time he jumped off a high roof, apparently trying to commit suicide. Bill showed increasing signs of depression. For example, he often lay on the sofa and talked about how he hated himself.

Because he was exhibiting suicidal behavior and his behavior was deteriorating, Bill was placed in a psychiatric hospital. He was given Haldol (haloperidol, an antipsychotic drug). The medication, combined with structured inpatient treatment, helped get his behavior under control. Bill went home after about two months. He continued his medication and got outpatient therapy as well. He went from the hospital to a highly structured behavioral program in a special class, where he and the other seven students got lots of individual attention and tutoring.

Bill was still a highly anxious and disorganized student. He was often described as out of touch with reality, bizarre, and silly. He was impulsive and had persistent problems paying attention. He had unpredictable mood changes and engaged frequently in daydreaming. His problems were most apparent during unstructured times, and the structure of the behavioral program appeared to help him control his behavior. In spite of his difficulties, Bill was said to be likable, popular with his classmates and teachers, intelligent, and curious.

When he was 15, Bill was taken off Haldol because he'd made steady improvement. He had no adverse effects when he was taken off the drug. He returned to his neighborhood high school, where he earned As and Bs. He made friends and was active in sports and other school activities. At age 17 he was a popular senior, editor of the school newspaper, and on the soccer team. At that age, he showed no signs of schizophrenia or other psychiatric illness, and he was planning to go to college.

Rewritten from Asarnow, Tompson, and Goldstein (1994)

Questions About the Case

1. Why do you think Bill's schizophrenia was not recognized immediately?
2. Had you been Bill's teacher in the early grades, what action would you have taken to address his problems?
3. In what ways is Bill's case typical and in what ways is it not typical of childhood schizophrenia?

Erin was diagnosed with schizophrenia as a child. Her case was introduced in the earlier section on conceptual models (Chapter 4). Here, she gives us a first-person description of what the experience is like.

Erin (Continued from Case on Biogenic Conceptual Model)

Yes, I was hearing voices. I first started hearing them when I was in the fourth grade. I was really sick then. At first the voices seemed friendly, but then they started seeming mean. They really scared me a lot. The voices got so bad that I couldn't even go into my bedroom. I couldn't go there because I was scared that a voice who seemed to live there might get me. After a while some of the voices I heard were good ones. They protected me from the bad voices. The good ones were the first to disappear, though, when I started taking medication. That's so weird, though, because when the medication took away the good voices I was scared of bad voices again.

This happened to me six years ago, so I really don't remember specific things that the voices said to me. I just remember that hearing the bad voices was very scary. The voices went with a bad headache, so the doctors took x-rays of my head to see if they could find anything wrong with my brain. They didn't find anything wrong.

I could even see the voices when I was really sick. Seeing them was very weird. They were like ghosts, and they were horrible. I remember that one of them had three heads. When I was in the hospital, I drew pictures of them. Some of them even had names, like "Greenie." The wallpaper in my bedroom is old-fashioned girls with bonnets. I used to think that these girls would come alive and come off the walls and attack me. That was pretty scary.

My psychiatrist told me not to think about the voices. So, whenever I felt like I was going to hear voices, I'd go to my mother. She could always tell I was having a bad time because I got big, dark circles under my eyes. She'd make me lie down and relax and tell me not to be distracted by the voices. What my mom did worked. Now the voices seem like a bad dream. I don't ever, ever want them to come back. Having schizophrenia is very painful.

The voices told me to jump out of the window of the hospital once. I didn't want to do what they said because I was on the sixth floor, and I was afraid of heights. I told my nurse about this, and she put me within constant sight of the nurses. This meant that I had to sleep on two chairs pushed together next to the nurse's station, but at least I felt safe there.

Rewritten from Anonymous (1994)

Questions About the Case

1. In what ways does Erin's case illustrate the pain of having schizophrenia?
2. Why is schizophrenia often not recognized immediately in children?
3. Had you been Erin's teacher at some point in her life, what could you have done that would have been most helpful?

15

Cases on Assessment

Sometimes it isn't clear whether problem behavior constitutes an emotional or behavioral disorder (EBD), and the distinction between normal difficulty and EBD is especially difficult if the child is young. The problem of differentiating EBD from other difficulties is made even more complicated by the student's response to intervention. If a child responds to early intervention, does that mean that he or she actually didn't have EBD or just that early intervention for EBD was successful? (Remember, too, that being found to have EBD doesn't necessarily mean that the student has been or should be identified for special education.) The case of Dean illustrates our point.

Dean

Three-year-old Dean was known as "Mean Dean" at our childcare center. Everybody at the daycare center knew when he got there in the morning, because there was always an "episode" when he arrived. For example, on the morning we're thinking of, Dean punched one of his peers during breakfast. Later that day he pushed a girl off the jungle gym. She fell and cut her face. The director of the program felt she couldn't control Dean's behavior, so she called his mom and told her Dean couldn't attend our school any more. We found out that he'd been expelled from two other childcare programs.

Dean's mother simply didn't know what to do next. She knew Dean was a really difficult kid, but she didn't have anywhere to leave him when she worked. She couldn't find babysitters who'd put up with him. She was afraid of leaving Dean with her other kids because of how explosive he was, and she was afraid he'd hurt them. He had screaming, kicking tantrums sometimes and refused to comply with her instructions.

So we decided to try to help. We thought a multidisciplinary evaluation was in order, so we got the results of a behavior rating scale, a developmental inventory, and an adaptive behavior scale. In addition, we did some behavioral observation and had his speech and language skills evaluated by a speech-language pathologist. After we looked at all this information, we explained to Dean's mother that, although he had only slight delays in cognitive and language skills, he was considerably delayed in social-emotional-behavioral skills. Our recommendation was that Dean get intensive intervention for his behavior and have some speech-language intervention, too, so that he would be able to communicate better.

Dean and his mother were lucky to live near an innovative preschool program that included interventions specifically designed for young kids with EBD. It was a program based on behaviorism, and the staff conducted a functional behavior analysis and required parents to attend a training program for at least the first month their child was enrolled. After attending this program for a month, Dean's behavior was much improved at school and at home. He learned how to get his teacher's and his mother's attention more appropriately. He also learned how to get along better with his peers. His misbehavior no longer got him what he wanted. After four months, he was able to go back to a more typical childcare center. He still got itinerant support services from a specially trained teacher.

Dean was able to go to a regular kindergarten. The kindergarten report was that he was getting along well with his peers and wasn't having significant problems.

Rewritten from Stichter, Conroy, and Kauffman (2008)

Questions About the Case

1. Do you think Dean has or had EBD?
2. What do you think would have happened to Dean if he had not received early intervention that addressed his problem behavior?
3. Do you think it was important to teach Dean's mother to work with his problem behavior? Why or why not?
4. Why do you think that not all school districts provide a comprehensive early intervention program targeted for young children with behavior problems?

Learning and behavioral problems are often intertwined, often to the extent that it is difficult to know whether one came first and created conditions for the other. Many students with EBD have very significant problems in academic learning, and many are labeled as having learning disabilities (LD) before being labeled as having EBD (and some students carry a combined label or are served in a special education program for both categorical groups). Regardless of the label the student receives, or even if the student receives no special education label at all, we still have the problem of how best to teach the student. Appropriate teaching starts with appropriate assessment of the problem, as the case of Larissa illustrates.

Larissa

Larissa was referred for evaluation for special education by her third-grade teacher. At age 8, she was noncompliant with requests, was oppositional, threatened her teacher with bodily harm, and was way behind her peers academically. She had a lot of difficulty with both reading and math. She also left the classroom without permission, especially during instruction. She'd developed a history of disciplinary referrals in the second grade, so her third-grade teacher didn't see the problem as a new one. In fact, Larissa had been referred for special education evaluation in the second grade, but she wasn't found eligible for learning disability (LD) or emotionally disturbed (ED) services. Bad, but not bad enough.

Larissa's parents didn't know what to do. The third-grade teacher met with them several times, and they told her how Larissa was difficult to manage at home. She often refused to do her homework, and she'd scream and lock herself in her bedroom if they prodded her. Her parents were concerned that she was falling further behind academically. The Child Study Team doing the evaluation on Larissa was concerned, too, and they noted that Larissa's behavior was a particular problem during instruction.

Surprisingly, Larissa was well liked by her peers, and she had some friends. The team doing the evaluation found that Larissa's IQ was in the low normal range. Although her math skills were in the low normal range, her reading skills were way below average. Her adaptive behavior and speech-language skills were below normal, too. Although in second grade her behavior wasn't in the "clinical" range, it was now, and the school psychologist noticed that she was significantly more disruptive and noncompliant than her peers. This time, the team found her eligible for ED services.

The decision of the committee was that Larissa ought to stay in a regular third-grade class for most of the day but go to a resource room for part of the day. The resource room provided her with intensive instruction in core academics, self-management, and social skills. The social skills instruction was given in a small group, and they worked specifically on management of anger and explosive behavior. Larissa continued to be a member of her regular class for things like lunch and special activities. Although her academic and social skills improved by the end of the year, the decision was that she should continue receiving the special services of the resource room.

Rewritten from Stichter, Conroy, and Kauffman (2008)

Questions About the Case

1. Which do you think came first—Larissa's learning problems or her behavior problems?
2. Would you classify Larissa as having LD or EBD? Would she need different services, depending on the label?
3. Should the evaluation have identified Larissa's disabilities earlier? If they had identified her earlier as needing special services, what should they have been, how should they have been delivered, and how might the outcome have been different?
4. Do you think there are other services that Larissa needs but is not getting? If so, what other services would you recommend?

Sometimes there seems to be no perceptible adversity in the life of a youngster with EBD. Then we wonder why the youngster is acting so badly because it appears to us that he or she has many advantages and little or nothing to complain about. If we try to put ourselves in the student's shoes, we think we would be very happy and behave very well—be happy and well adjusted. On closer inspection, however, we may find that the outward appearances of the youngster's life (e.g., family affluence) are deceiving—that he or she is really experiencing what we'd consider difficult circumstances, and we were simply unaware of them. But that's not always the case. Sometimes, we can't find an apparent reason for the problem in the youngster's life circumstances. We're just mystified. We might not even know where to start in doing an evaluation.

Mark

Mark sat on the other side of the table in my classroom. He seemed to be a hostile adolescent. He also seemed nervous or anxious about something. He fiddled with a pack of cigarettes, turning them over incessantly, as if his intense concentration on the pack of cigarettes would divert the staff's attention. He looked "preppy," not only with the cigarettes but with his unbuttoned blue oxford shirt, tan cords, and docksiders.

The first day of class, Mark got there early enough to get a favored seat—last desk in the row. He liked to wall himself off by keeping the back of his chair against the wall and strewing his possessions—books, paper, pencils, pens . . . all of his stuff—on the floor around him. He seemed to want attention but refuse it at the same time. He didn't want anyone invading his space, and he verbally abused anyone who touched him. He had a sophisticated wit, but he was outrageously vulgar and described how he'd get rid of his enemies (including me). He seemed to love putting people down, sometimes by putting them on. Once, when a slow student in my class marveled that Mark lived in the best section of town, Mark explained that sparkling water (a particular brand of it) came out of his faucets at home.

Mark portrayed himself as a victim at least once a day. Of course, I was the victimizer because I was his teacher. He considered my requests for his classwork irrational. He found my requests that he not use obscenities without merit. If I requested that he cooperate in some way, he considered that request untimely. And, after refusing to do what I asked, he'd describe the details of how he was going to get rid of me. He had a way of inventing new vulgarities and elaborating old ones with picturesque terms. One of the other staff members even started a dictionary of his barbaric terms. He got sent to time-out a lot, and although I spent hours trying to talk to him, all I got for my trouble was rejection—refusal of any verbal or physical contact.

As the end of school approached, Mark's nervous, compulsive, repetitive behavior got even worse. He seemed to be pacing in his mind even when he was sitting still. His mental gymnastics got even more irrational and painful.

Rewritten from Maruskin-Mott (1986)

Questions About the Case

1. If you were going to try to find out why Mark behaves as he does, how would you go about it? Supposing that you were going to conduct a functional behavioral assessment (FBA) for Mark, exactly what would you do?
2. If you were Mark's teacher, how would you have planned for his instruction? What ideas do you have about his individual education program (IEP)?

3. Supposing that you were to devise a positive behavioral intervention plan (BIP) for Mark, how would you go about it?
4. If you were trying to approach Mark as recommended by proponents of what's known as positive behavioral intervention and support (PBIS), what behavior would you encourage, support, or reinforce, and how would you do it?

REFERENCES

Anonymous. (1994). First person account: Schizophrenia with childhood onset. *Schizophrenia Bulletin, 20,* 587–590.

Asarnow, J. R., Tompson, M. C., & Goldstein, M. J. (1994). Childhood-onset schizophrenia: A follow-up study. *Schizophrenia Bulletin, 20,* 599–617.

Berkowitz, P. H. (1974). Pearl H. Berkowitz. In J. M. Kauffman & C. D. Lewis (Eds.), *Teaching children with behavior disorders: Personal perspectives* (pp. 24–49). Upper Saddle River, NJ: Merrill/Prentice Hall.

Carlson, P. (2003, January 26). The psychotic bank robber: A schizophrenic teen takes desperate measures. His parents want help. The law wants prison. *Washington Post,* F1, pp. F4–F5.

Carpenter, B., & Bovair, K. (1996). Learning with dignity: Educational opportunities for students with emotional and behavioral difficulties. *Canadian Journal of Special Education, 11*(1), 6–16.

Corwin, M. (1997). *And still we rise: The trials and triumphs of twelve gifted inner-city students.* New York: Perennial.

Dunlap, G., Robbins, F. R., & Kern, L. (1994). Some characteristics of nonaversive intervention for severe behavior problems. In E. Schopler & G. B. Mesibov (Eds.), *Behavioral issues in autism* (pp. 227–245). New York: Plenum.

Goor, M. B., & Santos, K. E. (2002). *To think like a teacher: Cases for special education interns and novice teachers.* Boston: Allyn & Bacon.

Hallahan, D. P., & Kauffman, J. M. (2006). *Casebook to accompany exceptional learners: Introduction to special education* (10th ed.). Boston: Allyn & Bacon.

Hodgkinson, H. L. (1995). What should we call people? Race, class, and the census for 2000. *Phi Delta Kappan, 77,* 173–179.

James, M., & Long, N. (1992). Looking beyond behavior and seeing my needs: A red flag interview. *Journal of Emotional and Behavioral Problems, 1*(2), 35–38.

Kamps, D. M., Leonard, B. R., Dugan, E. P., Boland, B., & Greenwood, C. R. (1991). The use of ecobehavioral assessment to identify naturally occurring effective procedures in classrooms serving students with autism and other developmental disabilities. *Journal of Behavioral Education, 1,* 367–397.

Kane, M. J. (1994). Premonitory urges as "attentional tics" in Tourette's syndrome. *Journal of the American Academy of Child and Adolescent Psychiatry, 33,* 805–808.

Kaslow, N. J., Morris, M. K., & Rehm, L. P. (1998). Childhood depression. In R. J. Morris & T. R. Kratochwill (Eds.), *The practice of child therapy* (3rd ed., pp. 48–90). Boston: Allyn & Bacon.

Kauffman, J. M. (2011). *Toward a science of education: The battle between rogue and real science.* Verona, WI: Attainment.

Kauffman, J. M., Hallahan, D. P., Mostert, M. P., Trent, S. C., & Nuttycombe, D. G. (1993). *Managing classroom behavior: A reflective case-based approach.* Boston: Allyn & Bacon.

Kauffman, J. M., Lloyd, J. W., Baker, J., & Riedel, T. M. (1995). Inclusion of all students with emotional or behavioral disorders? Let's think again. *Phi Delta Kappan, 76,* 542–546.

Kauffman, J. M., & Pullen, P. L. (1996). Eight myths about special education. *Focus on Exceptional Children, 28*(5), 1–12.

Kauffman, J. M., Pullen, P. L., Mostert, M. P., & Trent, S. C. (2011). *Managing classroom behavior: A reflective case-based approach* (5th ed.). Upper Saddle River, NJ: Pearson Education.

Klein, A., & Harris, H. R. (2006, April 25). Md. boy charged with murder: Police say 12-year-old bludgeoned mother and brother. *Washington Post*, pp. B1, B9.

Maruskin-Mott, J. (1986). Portrait of Mark Matthews. *Gifted/Creative/Talented, 9*(6), 53.

Mayo, T. (1839). *Elements of pathology of the human mind*. Philadelphia: Waldie.

McHugh, J. (1987, April 5). Portrait of trouble: Teen's crimes began early. *Daily Progress*, pp. A1, A6.

Noll, M. B., Kamps, D., & Seaborn, C. F. (1993). Prereferral intervention for students with emotional or behavioral risks: Use of a behavioral consultation model. *Journal of Emotional and Behavioral Disorders, 1*, 203–214.

Patterson, G. R. (1982). *Coercive family process*. Eugene, OR: Castalia.

Patton, J. R., Blackbourn, J. M., Kauffman, J. M., & Brown, G. B. (1991). *Exceptional children in focus* (5th ed.). Upper Saddle River, NJ: Merrill/Prentice Hall.

Rappaport, S. R. (1976). Sheldon R. Rappaport. In J. M. Kauffman & D. P. Hallahan (Eds.), *Teaching children with learning disabilities: Personal perspectives* (pp. 344–371). Columbus, OH: Charles E. Merrill.

Rothman, E. P. (1974). Esther P. Rothman. In J. M. Kauffman & C. D. Lewis (Eds.), *Teaching children with behavior disorders: Personal perspectives* (pp. 218–239). Upper Saddle River, NJ: Merrill/Prentice Hall.

Seiss, D. (2011, June 16). Whatever happened to . . . . the boy with ADHD? Retrieved July 2, 2011, from http://www.washingtonpost.com/lifestyle/magazine/whatever-happened-tothe-boy-with-adhd/2011/04/29/AGqWQ8XH_story.html

Serbin, L. A., Stack, D. M., Schwartzman, A. E., Cooperman, J., Bentley, V., Saltaris, C., & Ledhingham, J. (2002). A longitudinal study of aggressive and withdrawn children into adulthood: Patterns of parenting and risk to offspring. In R. J. McMahon & R. D. Peters (Eds.), *The effects of parental dysfunction on children* (pp. 43–69). New York: Kluwer.

Somashekhar, S. (2007, April 12). Two boys charged in blazes at 3 houses: Passersby alerted family in danger. *Washington Post*, pp. B1, B5.

St. George, D. (2011, February 20). Student's suspension furthered his despair. *Washington Post*, pp. A1, A16–17.

Stark, K. D., Ostrander, R., Kurowski, C. A., Swearer, S., & Bowen, B. (1995). Affective and mood disorders. In M. Hersen & R. T. Ammerman (Eds.), *Advanced abnormal child psychology* (pp. 253–282). Hillsdale, NJ: Erlbaum.

Stichter, J. P., Conroy, M. A., & Kauffman, J. M. (2008). *An introduction to students with high-incidence disabilities*. Upper Saddle River, NJ: Merrill/Prentice Hall.

Warner, J. (2010). *We've got issues: Children and parents in the age of medication*. New York: Riverhead Books.